How I Lived a Year on
Just a Pound a Day

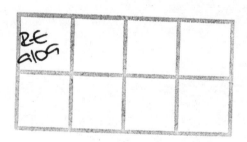

RE
9109

How I Lived a Year on Just a Pound a Day

Kath Kelly

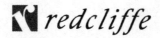

First published in 2008 by Redcliffe Press Ltd.,
81g Pembroke Road, Bristol BS8 3EA

Reprinted 2008, 2009

www.redcliffepress.co.uk
info@redcliffepress.co.uk

ISBN 978 1 906593 12 4

British Library Cataloguing-in-Publication-Data
A catalogue record for this book is available from the British
Library

Typeset by Harper Phototypesetters Ltd., Northampton, and
printed by HSW, Tonypandy.

Kath Kelly was broke. That was okay, as all her friends were too. But she had an important event to budget for, just a year away. How could she save enough in time, and still have some kind of a life in the process? One drunken night, she made a rash decision: to live on just one pound a day for the next twelve months.

This is the incredible but true story of how a mission to cut her spending to the bone showed one woman another side of herself and of human nature. Through the ups and downs of a year like no year she had spent before, she discovered how greed and waste was messing up people – to say nothing of the planet – and came to see how much fun can be had on a few pennies a day.

In for a Pound

I rashly decide to live on a pound a day (except for rent), and now I have to prove to my friends I can do it.

It was on my third glass of wine that inspiration came to me. Funny how often the world seems easy to put right about then.

'I know!' I announced. 'I'll live on a pound a day! For a year!'

This was greeted in silence by the knot of friends escaping the party noise in the courtyard. From inside the flat came the sound of glass breaking, followed by a volley of swearing.

Heather was staring at me owlishly over her gin and tonic. 'You want to *live* on a *pound a day* for a *year?*'

The others turned from her to me. 'That's impossible!' said Maunagh, whose birthday we were celebrating. 'What about drink?'

'It might be possible in Bangladesh or somewhere,' added Beverley kindly, 'but even the bus to town costs two quid, and it's only a mile away.'

'I think it can be done,' I asserted stubbornly. 'I'll walk, or ride my bike. And I know loads of places to get free food and drink.'

'Yeah, like here!' said Bern, offering me some of the expensive red he had brought. My bottle of Value Spanish Wine stood empty and reproachful on the table.

Crossly, I covered the glass with my hand. 'I'll do it without sponging. If I want to buy wine, I'll – I'll save up for a few days.'

Bern raised his eyebrows and poured himself a generous measure.

'Maybe you can *eat* on a pound a day,' said Tina, scoffing the last of her family-sized pack of Doritos, 'but what about clothes?'

'Shoes!' called prettily-shod Maunagh.

'You'd lose weight and have to get all new things,' said Beverley, 'because you'd have to be vegetarian.'

'You couldn't travel anywhere.'

'Or buy tampons. You'd have to wash out old rags.'

'No cinema or theatre.'

'What about going to the pub? You couldn't even have a quick coffee.'

My so-called friends had taken up my idea and run with it, all the way to the rubbish dump. I looked around the familiar faces and knew I had to prove them wrong.

Bern took a swig from his glass with flamboyant relish. 'You want to know what I think? After a couple of weeks you'd be so sick of the telly and the library, you'd go on a binge and max out the credit card.'

'I haven't even *got* a credit card,' I snapped. 'That's the whole point.' And with that I put down my glass and made up my mind.

We were all in financial strife at that party. Some of us had debts or near-impossible mortgages. Others had demanding children, or partners who acted like them. As for me, I wanted to save up. My brother's wedding was a year away, the following June, and I didn't want to get him a set of bath towels and a tea-cosy. So as we sat there in the sun at Maunagh's, bemoaning our money troubles even as we drank ourselves deeper into debt, I knew that now was the time to take drastic action. Could it be done? I had no idea. But making a pledge to live on a pound a day, just £365 for a whole year, in front of my closest mates, was the best way I could think of to give it a fair try.

The idea had seeded itself in my mind while watching the Richard and Judy show earlier in the year. They were interviewing an American woman, Judith Levine, who in 2004 realised she had spent over a thousand dollars in the run-up to Christmas, and resolved to buy nothing but necessities over the next twelve months. She had written a book, *Not buying it: a year without shopping,* which was a great success in the USA. The book described the year she and her partner spent in New York and their house in the country, shopping only for the things they felt they couldn't live without.

It was a good book (I read it over several days, without buying it, in the coffee shop of my favourite bookstore) and she had some fascinating points to make in challenging America's consumer culture. But her definition of 'necessities' certainly wasn't mine. I'd been skint for long enough to realise that nobody needs to spend $70 on a haircut, or to run two cars, or keep two houses, which Levine did throughout their 'year without shopping'. She allowed herself to spend whatever she wanted on food, though not on alcohol, and to travel as usual. Hardly living on the edge, I thought, as I read her smug accounts of resisting the temptations of Starbucks and designer jeans – most of the time. I was sure I could knock her abstemious year into a cocked hat, from my little rented room in a shared house in Bristol.

At the party the questions kept coming.

'What about your rent?'

'And bills?'

'What about if you got ill, or needed a dentist?'

'Would you still accept stuff from friends, like meals and presents? How would people feel about that?'

I had to confess I hadn't thought of some of those things, but the wine made me brave. So as darkness fell and the guests drifted home, my little clique talked the ground rules over. It would have to be a secret: if my brother found out, or my colleagues, or my family, they'd make sure I cheated. My friends at the party would be the only ones in the know. And now they were holding me to the challenge, there was no turning back.

June

Regretting a rash decision, meeting the challenge of cash-collection envelopes at work and showing my friends there IS such a thing as a free lunch ...

I woke the next morning with a pounding head and a desperate thirst. Thank goodness it's Sunday, was my first thought. I'll have a greasy fry-up at Lockside, read the papers and have a few cups of strong, strong coffee. I could call Heather and see if she's up for meeting there.

Like a second blow to the head, memory of the night before kicked in. What the hell had I let myself in for this time? Had my friends taken me seriously, or, I rather hoped, had they been too far gone to remember?

The strident bleeping of my phone sent another dart of pain through my skull. 'Morning!' said the text, 'Superdrug have special offer: 26p a pack on paracetamol!'

It was from Bern. 'Ha bloody ha,' I texted back. But just before I hit 'Send' I remembered it cost 10p to send a text on Pay as You Go. Ten per cent of today's expenditure!

It was more dignified to ignore him, I decided.

A shower and a couple of glasses of water improved my mood somewhat. Searching for something to wear, I noticed for the first time how *many* of everything I had: about twenty sets of underwear and socks, eight pairs of shoes, a couple of dozen tops. Some of them had never been worn. And I was someone who considered herself a very modest consumer, living in an extremely limited space, with a kettle and microwave nudging the bicycle and bed in my room. I took a pride in my austere lifestyle.

'Possessions? I don't value them,' I had often boasted. Well, that was clearly because I wasn't short of anything at all. Looking around, I noticed there were so many unused toiletries in my cupboard that the door wouldn't shut. And a lack-of-toilet-paper anxiety had prompted me to stock up with three bargain multipacks under my desk. Who was I to criticise Judith Levine's extravagances? I was beginning to get cross with myself in a hung-over, paranoid way.

The fridge and freezer reproached me with loads of stuff I'd forgotten all about. The food cupboard, though small, had duplicates of several things. OK, they were cheap brands or special offers mostly, but why did I buy them if they were still sitting there? And just how many jars of Indian lime pickle does one person need?

In the act of throwing the more out-of-date foods away, I changed my mind. I might be glad of them in a week or two, in date or not. And from the fridge there was enough of everything to knock up a decent cooked breakfast for Heather and me. No milk, but coffee and tea taste just the same without it, I maintained. And finishing an old crossword together was the same as buying a new one that Sunday. The *Daily Mail* isn't my newspaper of choice, but I decided that any reading matter in my landlady's clean-ish recycling bin was fair game for someone living on a pound a day.

One sunny evening not long afterwards, nursing a couple of dented cans of beer (reduced price: 20p each) I was telling Maunagh about an article I'd read in that *Mail*.

'But I spend nowhere near that much!' she exclaimed, as I told her about the £289 a week – £15,028 a year – that women aged between 21 and 25 are supposed to spend.

'It sounded like a lot to me too,' I agreed, 'until I remembered you telling me about the Chanel perfume you bought last week, and the outfit for that date, and the taxi home on Thursday night…'

'Well, some of those are essentials,' she broke in. 'If I hadn't got a taxi I could have been mugged, and lost my best bag and all my money as well…'

'It's fine if you're happy spending that,' I said, 'but you stress every month about where it's all gone, and promise yourself you won't do it next time.'

'I know,' she sighed. 'I just love having lovely things around me. It's what I *do*.'

From my backpack I fished out the article, and we went through the alleged weekly spend. The women surveyed spent on average £82 on clothes, accessories and shoes, £46 on makeup and toiletries, £7 on hairdressing and £64 on alcohol and socialising.

'Actually, that's not that hard to do,' admitted Maunagh.

'I was spending £19 a week on my mobile, easily, before I started doing this pound thing,' I said.

'£10 on music? That's not much at all really,' she replied. 'And if you buy a couple of magazines and papers it can soon add up to £8 a week.'

We agreed that the figures could well be right: £19 a week on holidays, £25 on treats and presents, £12 on cinema trips or DVDs.

'But there's no need. They could be saving for their own

home or getting a pension fund started with that kind of money, instead of getting into debt.'

'I know: an average of £3,830 each a year on credit card debt. It's scary.'

'But I feel like I owe myself something nice. It's like the hair advert – because I'm worth it!' said Maunagh.

'Especially at the end of a hard day. I mean, we're not in our twenties, but we only earn as much as they say they do here – less than that for me, even. I can't imagine earning eighteen grand a year!

'It's just so *boring*, being realistic,' Maunagh sighed. 'I want my things to be *nice*.'

'That's the trouble, isn't it?' I agreed. 'We all think we're worth more than our earning power. It's just how to feel worth it without having to spend money to prove it.'

'You're doing pretty well so far, aren't you?' said Maunagh. 'Have you cheated yet?'

'No, it's been easy up to now. The cupboard's still got stuff in it, and while the weather's nice we can sit outside just like we're in the pub.'

We looked across at the punters on the waterfront steps outside the Cottage. Their rounds of drinks had cost them considerably more than 20p, for sure.

'I didn't think you were much of a hoarder. You always say you don't like possessions.'

I fiddled with my can sheepishly. 'I know. But you should have seen how much stuff I'd forgotten I had, stashed away in my room.'

I told her about the clothes and shoes, the groceries and frozen goods still waiting to be used.

8

'They say the same here,' she said, pointing at the article again. 'It says they've got 30 tops, 29 knickers – I've got more than that – 25 pairs of shoes, 16 pairs of trousers, 14 bras and 13 skirts. Each!'

'I feel a bit better now,' I said. 'I thought eight pairs of shoes was bad enough, then I found these sandals and made it nine!'

'Eight handbags, six coats, five scarves and four hats...' Maunagh read on. 'I don't think that's very many, really. Not if you go out a lot.'

'Well, I've certainly got enough of everything for two years, not one,' I said.

'But they'll all be out of fashion!' She looked appalled.

'Since when have I been a fashion victim? I think I'll start my own trend: threadbare chic.'

For the first time Maunagh looked seriously concerned. 'You can borrow anything you want from me, you know.' She drained her can of beer and tried to set it down on the flagstones, but it was too dented to stay upright. 'How about another one at the Cottage now? My treat, of course.'

I laughed. 'You're your own worst enemy,' I said. 'Thanks, but you promised not to buy me drinks and coffees, remember? Come on, let's walk round the harbour and watch the sun go down.'

'Do you want to sign Andrew's card?' My boss leaned across the staff room with an envelope. 'His birthday's tomorrow.'

'Oh, er, sure.' I took the envelope, which jingled as I opened it. Inside was a card, which I duly signed, and a fair

9

bit of loose change for his gift. We only gave token presents to each other at the school where I worked, but it was the gesture that counted. I'd never really noticed before how many times we passed an envelope around, though. There was something every week: if not a birthday, it was a new baby or somebody ill, or sponsorship for some charity event. There were only twenty-five or so of us, including the office staff, and in the past I'd always put in a pound coin without thinking. But now I had both to watch every penny and still have something on me, just in case a collection came round.

From my suspiciously light purse I took two 20ps and added them to the kitty. I felt pretty mean. Nobody at work knew about my pound a day challenge – yet. I had resolved to tell them after six months, to see if they had noticed, and if they had, what it was that gave it away. I still had to appear professional and well dressed in front of the students. Luckily, teachers can get away with a bit of sartorial eccentricity, and teaching English to foreigners helped. They were more accepting of my behavioural foibles than British teenagers would have been.

I work part-time, but have to be on call in case anyone phones in sick. That suits me very well; I've always valued time more than money. But for this year it meant that I had to keep my mobile working and topped up, and my wardrobe halfway respectable. And there would be no taxis to rush me to school to cover an emergency. I had to rely on my bike, and avoid straying too far from Clifton – the Bristol suburb where I worked – during working hours. It was all about being well prepared, I'd decided.

Stephen came back from the shops with a bag of chips. The smell filled the room, prompting some of the others to take out their sandwiches, sold every breaktime in the common room. The cheapest one was two quid.

From my bag I produced a margarine tub. Inside were the remains of last night's pasta with tinned tomatoes and stir-fried cabbage. It looked a lot less appetising today, with the pasta shells' texture no longer *al dente*, but rather gelatinous and overblown. Heroically, I refused a chip and settled down to eat my bargain lunch cold. If only we had a microwave. And a fridge. It was going to get a bit tedious, always carrying a packed lunch, trying to plan the day around flasks and lunchboxes and reduced-price bread. Little by little, my reserves in the freezer had dwindled. My section of it was now filling up with 10p loaves at the end of their sell-by date, and the dog-ends of other meals in recycled containers, marked with labels such as 'bit of stir-fry' and 'beans, kidney and baked'. Leftovers were already my staple diet. Whereas before I'd mostly ignored the little gifts to the staff brought in by students who were leaving, now I looked forward to dates from Dubai, pickled plums from China or dry bean cakes from Taiwan. They were a welcome change from my rather monotonous lunchtime fare.

The same applied to school events: we were required to join the students on social outings every term, unpaid but with the incentive of a free drink or two or a ticket to a musical or play. I'd done my share in the past, but now I scanned the list eagerly, looking for things I could no longer go to on a pound a day. Would my colleagues notice a sudden change in my attitude to the social programme, or speculate about my new enthusiasm for Korean spicy cabbage and dried seaweed?

There were coach trips a couple of times a month too. Rich, the organiser, sold tickets to London, Oxford, Cambridge, Stratford and other places of interest. We were not required to attend, but if there were free seats, he was pleased to have teachers along. I signed up for several weekend excursions, and again wondered if this would excite any comment. I thought it would be a great way to explore galleries and museums once the novelty of those in Bristol had worn off. Also, my brother lived in Cambridge with his fiancée. I wanted to pop in on them from time to time as normal, so they wouldn't guess that I was following a new regime in order to save up for their wedding present. If a trip was cancelled due to low ticket sales, I would no doubt be bitterly disappointed. But it was high summer, it was easy to survive out of doors, and for the time being at least there was plenty to do. I cycled over to Bath, taking advantage of the light evenings, and watched incredible street performances in the Bath Fringe Festival. There was loads to see in the area, and I did my best to persuade my students to take advantage of it in the short time they had in the country. Don't people say that if you live in a place, you take its attractions for granted? Well, I was out to prove them wrong.

'Come to library – free cake!' ran my email to all of my friends who were around. It was the hundredth birthday of the Central Library, and the Mayor was there giving a speech. We were all attending for the champagne and nibbles, and having a jolly good time courtesy of our fine

City Council. Thank goodness for free internet access! Although Bern had teased me about all the time I'd be spending in the library, I had actually found it indispensable. It wasn't because of the books, which I still dipped into for free in bookshops, or to retreat from the weather – it was high summer after all – but for the internet. It was absolutely vital for keeping in touch with people once phone calls became a luxury and stamps too. Ignoring the sad image Bern had fostered of my joining the knot of down-and-outs dozing over the periodicals, I popped in most days to search for free events and to send messages.

Neil was the first to arrive as he was working from home that day.

'You seem to be managing all right then!' he said, nursing a glass in one hand and his baby son in the other. 'I've saved quite a bit as well, since we started doing lunch like this instead of in the pub.'

'So far, so good,' I agreed. 'There's lots to do in town if you look out for it.'

We were standing by the events noticeboard. I'd made notes in my diary about upcoming stuff: art openings, public lectures, concerts for free...

'So you're finding plenty to keep you busy. But what else are you going to have to show for it, if you do manage to get through a whole year like this?'

I looked at him over my paper plate. 'Well, it's not just a matter of spending only £365 in a year, aside from rent. I'd like to show people that it's possible to save up for something special and still have a good time in the process. And then there's so much surplus and excess and waste and

greed everywhere... I think I want to show that up as well.'
'Yeah, having the kids has really made us think about that,'
he said, jogging Finn up and down. 'We get all their stuff
from charity shops and it goes right back there a few weeks
later. And our parents will keep on buying them more and
more plastic crap, and we've got nowhere to put it. Babies
don't appreciate it anyway.'

'I know. The world just can't keep on living like that. We
should be more like your boys – they don't need new stuff
every five minutes to be happy.'

Finn began to squirm and wail. 'Short attention span
though!' said Neil ruefully. 'Don't suppose you'll be in the
pub this weekend, then?'

'No, don't think I will. Looks like you two are making
leaving noises, eh? But let's do lunch like this again!'

A few nights later, we had a drink together after all, in a
bookshop sampling local beers, the subject of the book
being launched. What with events like these and my school
soirées, managing with no money for drinks at least had not
yet been a problem, despite the issue of not being able to
buy rounds in a pub. But Neil had made me think. What
was my ultimate goal through this insane mixture of
hedonism and stinginess?

I got the chance to consider the answer thanks to a
postcard in the window of my local shop. 'Life coach in
training is looking for clients for a series of free sessions in
Redland. Call Lilli...' Well, I could hardly turn it down,
could I?

'What we do is talk about a list of goals for you. It could
be in your working life, your personal life or something

else. Maybe you'd like to be better organised financially, or have different living circumstances, for instance.' Lilli was a tall, well-groomed blonde. Her office was as immaculate as she was: even the flowers in their vase and the fruit in its bowl had been thoughtfully and precisely arranged.

'Hmm, I think I need to look at all of those,' I agreed, helping myself to more water from a cut-glass jug with tinkling ice.

I was hot and bothered from rushing to our first meeting. Somehow I'd guessed it wasn't a good idea to turn up late to see the person who was going to help you use your time better. But Lilli wasn't judgemental. I sensed she was kind and broad-minded, even if I wasn't the kind of business-woman who would pay her £40 or £50 an hour once she was qualified.

'We'll agree on a plan, and every week you'll have some homework. Can you commit to twelve one-hour sessions before October, and do homework as well?'

'I'd better do. I make my students do it, after all, so I should practise what I preach!' Absently I re-folded the sleeves of my crumpled blouse. I was scruffy and slack, I decided. And living on a pound a day was no excuse for not doing the ironing.

Later that evening, I stared up at the stars and thought about our meeting. We'd made a list of targets for the week, and I was already beginning to regret it. I'd promised to make an appointment at the bank to discuss my savings plan for the year, which was sure to be tedious. I seemed to have some kind of aversion to dealing with money, which stopped me from ever having any to speak of. Perhaps my challenge would help me to behave more like a grown-up by this time next summer.

Fat chance, I thought, stretching out on my rug on the grass. All around me were other irresponsible poor people, lying in the park late at night at Ashton Gate. I closed my eyes and wondered what it would be like to be homeless. OK in the summer, perhaps, but not a great option on the whole…

> *I'll tip my hat to the new constitution,*
> *Take a bow for the new revolution,*
> *Smile and grin at the change all around….*
> *We won't get fooled again!*

Inside the football stadium across the road, the crowd was going wild. Outside in the park, hundreds of others like me enjoyed The Who playing live for free. It was a beautiful night. The scent of the gardens drifted on the wind along with the heady smell of somebody's marijuana. I smiled to myself in the dark. My life coach was going to have her work cut out with me.

July

I learn to travel around on a pound a day, take up hitch-hiking again, get back into camping and buy very carefully.

'What do you think you're doing, out here on your own?'

'Has your car broken down, love?'

'I'm not going far, but I'll take you to the bus station in town if you want.'

'I never pick up hitch-hikers, but when I saw a woman on her own, I just felt I had to stop. There's all kinds of nutters out there, you know.'

'You're the first hitcher I've seen in years! Does it still work then?'

'Aren't you scared, hitching all by yourself?'

These are just a few of the comments I was treated to when I got back into hitch-hiking. I was a teenager in the Seventies when I first discovered this liberating mode of transport. I went everywhere by thumb, on my own, and apart from being propositioned by some decidedly unattractive, well, propositions, it always went well. Before deciding to live on a pound a day, it was still my default mode of transport. If it was too slow, too expensive or just too boring to go on a bus or a train, I'd write up a sign and get out to Gordano service station or Cribbs Causeway on a local bus, and start hitching. I met nice people and generally did very well. Of course, in those days I had the safety-net of a cashcard and a few quid in my wallet, plus credit on my mobile and the option of a taxi if it all went horribly wrong.

Now, I could either walk to the outskirts of Bristol, or cycle and hide my bike somewhere. Apart from for a day trip, I was reluctant to do the latter in case my bike was stolen. Five or six miles on foot, carrying luggage for the weekend, adds considerably to the journey time, so I gave up on Cribbs Causeway. Instead I walked over the Suspension Bridge and out of town to the west. Gordano Services got to know me well, and more than once I was picked up by someone who had given me a lift before. Sometimes I told the story of my pound-a-day year, sometimes not, depending on the driver's curiosity. If they were in the majority who had once hitched themselves before coming upon better times, they often exclaimed about my *still* hitching. Did they mean still, in this day and age, in the twenty-first-century? Or were they talking about my own middle-age and expressing surprise that someone as old as me was still behaving like a student? It was often hard to tell. Anyway, as long as they were *still* picking up strangers by the roadside, I didn't particularly care.

It's much harder to hitch-hike these days for many reasons (and maybe being in my forties is one of them, but I hope not). Motorways merge into one another without roundabouts or other setting-down places for the hitcher. A-roads are bigger and faster, and the traffic going the way you want may be in the lane on the other side of the road from where you are obliged to stand. Slip-roads less commonly have a hard shoulder or other pulling-in place. That makes it more difficult for a kind driver to stop and pick you up without being rear-ended for his or her trouble. Students almost always have cars, so they have no need to hitch. A whole generation lost to the cause! Soldiers and other servicemen are forbidden to hitch in uniform. And now, a lot of lorry drivers are forbidden to pick up passengers for insurance or security reasons.

Because of all this, hitching is now viewed less as an alternative activity and more as a deviant one, which is a shame. I felt that part of my motivation for surviving on a pound a day was to show up selfishness and greed. Insisting on driving a 5-seater car all by yourself is as silly as buying beyond your means 'because you're worth it'. It doesn't seem very green to demand such a lot of space, adding your own private carbon emissions to an overcrowded world.

People are scared of each other, too. I could be *anybody*, there by the roadside, couldn't I? And a few unfortunate horror movies have made the fear of both hitcher and hitchee even worse. Luckily, there are still people around who are prepared to share their trip, and they have found that everybody wins when they do so. It's great not having to own a car: cheaper, healthier and less stressful. And meeting someone in a car is a great way to break up the time, divide the driving, and augment the experience of a journey.

The world of the hitch-hiker has begun to go high-tech. There are internet sites such as Rideshare or Freewheelers which offer people the chance to register their journey as one-off or regular, and try to match driver and hitcher. Sometimes a contribution for petrol changes hands. Other possibilities include Gumtree, which offers a noticeboard facility for drivers or people hoping for a lift. The trouble is, it's worth the while of the hitchers to go online, but not for the people who are already in possession of the car keys…

With drivers, I've chatted about the pros and cons of introducing picking-up places on major roads, where people could pause to see if anyone needs a lift. But guess what? We have them already. They're called service stations, and back in the old days there'd be a queue of people at the exit waiting patiently with their signs. I hope they come back when petrol prices go up still higher and passenger lanes are introduced on the motorway.

One weekend I set off to visit my friend in Cornwall. Straight after work, I changed into my jeans and trainers and shouldered my day-pack. It contained a few clothes, waterproofs (even in July), a couple of sandwiches and some bargains from a Bristol supermarket: cheese, pork pies and muffins, all frozen when I set off, destined to be thawed by arrival. These were my contributions to my friend's larder; nothing had cost more than 10p at the end of the day before it went out of date. I was getting pretty good at bargain-hunting in the shops just before closing time, and going out with food and clothes for every eventuality.

My first sign said 'Exeter' and a chatty businesswoman took me all the way to the services there. I drank a (free) cup of hot water in the café. Then I waited down by the petrol pumps with a new sign, 'Truro' in marker-pen block capitals inside a plastic wallet. And waited. And waited. I ate a sandwich and moved to a different spot. Lots of drivers smiled or shrugged. One or two gave me the thumbs-up to impress their friends, or yelled something like 'A ride for a ride!' out of their window. Very funny. Then at last a taxi driver pulled up, an elderly man with his blue-rinsed wife beside him. They had passed on a hospital patient from their taxi to another at the services; someone who had broken his leg while on a coach holiday. They were happy to take me down to Truro, where I easily got my last lift, a kind man who had been working nearby and who went the long way home to drop me in my friend's village. The trip had taken four hours and cost nothing.

I went to the same place five times over my year: in the pouring rain or fog or sunshine, sometimes quickly, sometimes slowly. But I was always safe and each time was an adventure, meeting new people with lots to talk about and giving someone the warm glow that comes from doing a favour to a stranger, just because you can.

It was true, what Bev had said about buses in Bristol. They were overpriced and hopelessly unreliable. It was less annoying to just walk it. I'd read somewhere that changing your shoes frequently helped them to last longer, so I kept a pair at work and swapped again every time I came home. They had to last all year, and I was doing a lot of miles around the city these days. Thank goodness for my trusty bicycle, too. Cycling was a passport to other things as well: at the Biggest Bike Ride in June I socialised with the rest of the two-wheeled community and got free maps, samples and entertainment after a great trip around the city together. Then there was Bike to Work Day. That was even better: my bike was serviced for free by the Bike Doctors (a team from local bike shops). I had my blood pressure and heart rate checked, and then, just to get the cholesterol back up, I joined the queue for a breakfast provided by Ikea. Apart from the bacon butties and cereal, there was delicious fruit, which kept me going through another long hot day at school. Summer in the city was kicking in, and I planned another long weekend on a pound a day.

My trip to Cornwall had gone very well, and my friend hadn't guessed a thing. But now the weather was baking hot, and I wanted to get out of the city again for some fresh air. I decided to hitch to Swansea. Part of the reason I chose Wales as my destination was because English people were getting into a frenzy about the football, and I wanted to avoid anything to do with it. My luggage was heavier than I liked to carry: my tiny green tent and summer-weight sleeping bag were okay, but once I'd been to the giant Tesco in Swansea I would be really laden. Four litres of water was the minimum to take to my camping-place, I reckoned, and I'd carry another bottle and fill it when possible during the day. Of course, even the cheapest campsite was out of the question, but I had a couple of secret locations in mind where nobody would spot me if I didn't light a fire or make any noise.

I'd done a lot of camping in my twenties, but have to admit I've gone a bit soft in recent years. I find guest-house beds and en-suite bathrooms rather more appealing than backpacking with heavy equipment while pitting myself against the unpredictable elements. I hoped a weekend trying to get comfy on the hard ground wouldn't put me off for life.

The food for three days had to be very cheap, easy to carry and non-perishable. I loitered in the delicious cool of the supermarket, scanning and re-scanning the shelves. Could I fit the bill with my precious three quid, hoarded away over the previous week? One of the ground rules for the year was that I mustn't get into the red, but could save from days where I spent less than a pound. Right-oh, cream crackers, 18p. Biscuits, ditto. A couple of loose carrots to eat raw, 20p. Reduced apples, 30p. Over-ripe bananas at 30p a kilo, 18p. I might regret those later when they got all squashed, I thought, but I had to have a bit of fresh stuff. That's a pound and 4p gone. Now, two tins of sardines for 42p. Peanuts, 24p. Cheese reduced to £1.99 a kilo! Fantastic. 200g for 40p. I already had one of my store of frozen 10p loaves from Bristol in my bag, and now I'd have some nice sandwiches. I splashed out on a lettuce for 19p and a couple of tomatoes, 23p. Just 90p left now… There was a ready meal of curry and rice, reduced, which I could afford, but would I like it cold? Nah. Okay, a can of bangers and beans and a mini quiche on its sell-by date. In the queue at the checkout, I double-checked my maths. It would be embarrassing to have forgotten to add something in. Well, it was fine in terms of price, but easy to carry? Not very. And non-perishable? What was I thinking, getting bananas and lettuce? They'd be stewed in the tent in no time.

Not to worry, I reflected, filling my water bottles at the sink in the toilets. The weight of the stuff wouldn't matter once I arrived. Most of it could be stashed out of sight while I went off during the day. I drank deeply while I had the chance, then packed the water too. Might as well get going then. I lifted my pack and staggered under its bulk.

I really hoped someone would pick me up before I walked too far…

It was easy. A soldier on leave stopped almost immediately, probably out of sympathy for my burden, and took me to within a couple of miles of my chosen beach. No hurry now: it was only Friday afternoon, beautiful weather and hardly a soul around yet. I left half my luggage a mile off the road and laboured over the sand dunes with the rest, then relayed back. It was hard going, uphill on loose sand, but well worth it. I was tucked away among the bushes on a shelf in the cliffs, with the sea whispering below on an almost empty golden beach. I sat back against my pack and sighed with pleasure. I had a book, an earphone radio and some fast-rotting fruit. What more could a woman want? Of course, the book was from the library, on the subject of frugal living. I wrote up my diary too, and pondered on my year's undertaking. There were lessons I had to learn. Lilli had already shown me that money wasn't necessary to achieve most of the goals I had set myself. I wanted to be more efficient and organised, using my time to the best advantage. Getting to that point, as she reminded me, was mostly a question of making an effort. I had to approach work and play with the right attitude, showing my friends that they were important to me even if we no longer went to restaurants or nightclubs. I resolved to show my family and colleagues too that I valued them. Even if it was harder work on a pound a day, that effort would be well spent.

The weekend went far too fast. I slept well through the sultry nights and rose early to swim. Each morning I

24

dismantled the tent in case some nosy dog-walker found my hidey-hole, and hauled my pack high into a tree with a rope, so it was hidden. With just enough for the day, I'd set off walking. The empty water bottle was filled and refilled, and used as a shower more than once. I luxuriated in my solitude, watching people on the beach come and go, and was sad on Sunday afternoon to pack up every trace of my presence and head back to Bristol. The thinking time had been important: I felt refreshed and newly inspired to keep going on my pound-a-day challenge. My goals were clearer to me and I had discovered yet more reasons to continue. A weekend on a beautiful beach, far away from anywhere where money could be spent even if I had some, was at least as good as any holiday I'd ever had before. And anyone could do it! Whatever your age or income, such pleasures are in everybody's reach.

August

Disaster strikes when I lose my bike, I discover the consequences of never refusing free food, get loads of good advice, and narrowly avoid becoming a 'dumpster diver'.

The cable lay like a dead snake, chopped in half. It was still twisted, as if it had put up a fight in its death throes, but its mortal blow had come from something very strong and sharp. I picked it up and saw the fibres neatly severed under the rubber exterior, the lock untouched. No sign of its best friend the D-lock, or their inseparable companion, my mountain bike.

What crime of passion had occurred out here while I was pottering innocently in the library? The love triangle between my three possessions had been violently broken. The snake's hold had been strong, but ultimately not strong enough. Were the D-lock and bike still clamped close together, hitching a ride on some mysterious journey in the back of a van, or had they too been split up? Perhaps even now someone else was having a free ride on that feckless bike.

I turned up my collar and set off on foot to work. What a pain. Bikes got stolen every day in Bristol, of course, but outside the library, in broad daylight with two locks attached, I thought it would be safe. Up the hill, through the university, marching so as not to be too late, the implications began to set in. No bike to go to Bath at the

weekend, no way of carrying heavy stuff back from the
cheaper supermarkets on the edge of town, no safe and
swift going home late at night when drunks prowled the
streets looking for trouble. *so TRUE*

I couldn't get taxis instead, or buses, or another bike, on
a pound a day. My temper rose against whatever scally it
was who had ruined my day, if not the rest of the year. I
was only a few weeks into my spending challenge and
stuffed already! I undid my jacket and stomped hot and
bothered into work to phone the police and report the
theft.

A couple of weeks later someone from the constabulary
phoned me, just to let me know they hadn't found my bike.
Nice of them to bother, I supposed. By then Heather had
lent me her very expensive Dawes bike as a replacement,
though I didn't dare let it out of my sight. It was festooned
with a length of chain and a chunky padlock, as well as the
locks it came with. I watched it through shop windows as
anxiously as a mother checks her sleeping baby. Still, it was
great to be able to get around as before, though I sometimes
left it at home at night to keep it safe, and took my chances
out there with the drunks.

One of those nights, I was plodding through Clifton after
a night round at a friend's place. I still caught myself
checking bikes being ridden past or chained to racks, just
hoping that one day I'd spot my own sadly missed steed. It
wasn't expensive or anything – £60 in Halford's sale – but
it was mine to trash or get nicked as I pleased.

That night I was taking a short cut down a leafy footpath.
Not an ideal safety measure, but I hadn't been home since

morning and I was worn out. The street lamp halfway down had been smashed again. Sugary crystals of glass crunched underfoot. I hoped there was no dog mess to tread in.

Against the railing leaned a bike. Silver grey, like mine had been, with front suspension. Surely it wasn't... No, as I looked closer I saw it was a different, superior make. But what a stupid place to lock it up at night!

With a jolt of surprise I saw it wasn't locked at all. Two flat tyres, but nothing else seemed wrong with it. They'll be lucky if it's still there tomorrow, I thought, turning for home.

But there it was on my way to work in the morning, and in the evening too. I hesitated, then knocked on the door of the house nearest the lane, to ask if anyone knew whose it was. 'They're always dumping stuff down there,' said the woman of the house. 'Probably stolen.'

So the next day I decided to be a good citizen. Maybe the karma would store up so nothing else of mine got nicked. I dragged the flat-tyred bike into town to the central police station I had phoned so recently. It had inexplicably closed down. Great. On then to the even more distant new police station, where I spent a tedious hour queuing, explaining myself and form-filling.

'...and if no-one claims it within six weeks, you can come back and take it if you want,' the desk officer added as she ripped apart the triplicate carbon copies.

'If I want! Of course I do!' Suddenly my urge to do the right thing had become worthwhile. I put a capitalised entry into my diary and hurried off, smiling, on the long walk back to work.

So there was a happy ending after all. The bike duly became mine, a nice bloke I know helped me fix it, my friend got her un-stolen expensive one back and I ended up with a better mode of transport than I started with. There must be something in that karma business.

But as for my old bike and the D-lock, they were never seen again. I hope you're happy together, wherever you are. And as for the cable, it's still really cut up.

I had fully expected to get fit during my austerity year: all that cycling and walking, no meals out or impulse buys of treats on the way home. I'd also scored a lot of trial days at gyms around the city. It was quite a luxury to be able to swim or take a sauna after work, even if I had to cycle a few miles for the privilege. It helped me to bear the August heat and go home refreshed. Before my challenge started, I'd cancelled my membership to Cannons gym in order to save money, and I missed it a lot. Luckily, they often offered open days and free trial tickets in the papers to attract new members. I took full advantage of those to check out the old place and to say hello to the regulars. They just thought I was being a bit lazy, not using the gym every day as before, and I didn't disabuse them of the idea.

One humid day, drying myself in the luxurious mirrored changing rooms of the Marriott hotel after trying out their beautiful colonnaded swimming pool, I caught sight of my reflection. My new haircut with highlights was an improvement, and Lilli approved of my greater attention to personal grooming. Of course, it was entirely free, at a trendy salon on Park Street, modelling for a young man who was hoping for a job there. His prospective boss was impressed enough with his work on me to offer him the position, and I felt oddly proud to have helped him. Numerous other places offered free or almost-free hair-dressing with their trainees, so that was one more advantage I already had over Judith Levine and her $70-a-time coiffure habit…

But the mirror told me some bad news too. I was putting on weight! Partly this was due to my policy of never refusing free food: if there was sampling going on in the shops, I was in there. Fresh and Wild provided me with a very reliable snack stop thanks to their tasters, and they were right next door to the gym… I cut coupons in papers lifted from recycling boxes. They often yielded advertise-ments about what was being given away by stores on a particular day. In the city centre or the shopping mall, stuff was often handed out as a promotion. I always made a point of going round twice: one for now and one for later! I had a stash of cereal bars, chewing gum, fizzy drinks, sweets and biscuits. Not exactly healthy stuff.

It was harder work still getting my 'five a day' of fruit and vegetables though. In the supermarkets, in terms of calories per penny, it was so much better value to get a packet of digestive biscuits (18p) than one orange (18p too.) It quickly became clear why there is more obesity among the poorer sector of the British population. That packet of biscuits would fulfil half the calorie needs of the average person for a day, and with some cheese spread or something at under 40p, would be quick, cheap and easy to carry to work. If I tried to get fresh and healthy foods, I found them much more expensive, heavy to carry on foot and requiring many extra trips to the shops, because of their perishability.

I had to eke out my food supplies as long as possible while eating healthily. I'd never given this much thought before, but under the circumstances I had to cook for maximum nutritional and monetary value to make my supplies last. When we walked over to the St. Marks Road street party to watch the parade and join in the dancing, I begged my friends for advice. Between them they came up with some great ideas.

Neil said I should never add salt to dried beans when soaking them: it makes the skins tougher and then they take longer to cook. He recommended keeping red cabbage in the dark, where it would remain fresh for a week or more, and using it for slow-cooking recipes like casseroles as well as eating it raw or steamed. He even offered the spoils of his allotment, but I politely declined. A good couple of tips from a lifelong veggie, though.

Maunagh had loads of ideas. She told me that stir-frying in a wok uses very little oil. A hand blender turns leftover or 'turning' fresh stuff into soups, or fruit smoothies with lots of crushed ice and no sugar. Herbs and spices add interest to 'samey' dishes: the same big pot of ingredients can be divided up and transformed into bolognese, curry and chilli con carne. Cooking onions with the meat saves using separate oil, and when making lasagne, the white sauce can be made with half milk, half water and cornflour instead of butter, milk and flour. Flavoured with parmesan, mustard and cayenne pepper, this has a tasty, cheesy appearance and flavour without adding more than a smidgeon of real grated cheese on the top. The lasagne can

31

have layers of spinach as well as pasta, and all kinds of vegetables in the tomato sauce, including broccoli stem and cauliflower leaves, to bulk it up into a bigger and more satisfying creation.

Bev's two penn'orth was that tinned or frozen fruit and veg. were often cheaper than fresh ones; they could go in salads or soups and stews for extra colour and quantity. She was right, I found: sweetcorn, tinned tomatoes or tinned peaches were very cheap indeed in the 'own brand' incarnation.

Helen told me to freeze foods as soon as they are cool, and get already frozen purchases back into the freezer fast. Getting whatever you didn't finish eating into the freezer keeps you away from temptation too! She advised packing stuff in portion-sized quantities to save wastage, and keeping the freezer tidy so it just takes a moment to grab something out and shut the door again. Same with the fridge. Label it all, keep all leftovers, and when you get a loaf home, halve it and put half straight in the freezer. I liked her advice.

Someone I met while hitching, the produce manager at a local supermarket, told me to separate fruit from veg. in storage as they contain different levels of ethylene, which hastens the rotting or ripening process. He said I should take everything out of plastic bags and put it in newspaper or cardboard boxes, as spread out as possible, in a cool, dark place. Garlic and onions keep best in the cupboard, provided it's well ventilated. He also said I should 'face up' my cupboard with the oldest stuff at the front, and transfer dry stuff from packets, once opened, into dry, airtight jars, writing the 'use by' date on a label.

Daphne pointed out that regular snacks make you feel less hungry, so I would be less likely to blow the day's budget on chocolate! I learned quickly always to carry something to eat. She also reminisced about how her mother would leave the peel or outside leaves on vegetables whenever possible to avoid wasting anything; what was discarded fed the hens which gave the family's eggs. Since most of the goodness in root vegetables is just under the skins, I thought this was a good point, and I wished I had a back garden big enough to keep a few hens!

I set off on my frequent trips to the shops with my own bags. Incinerating plastic uses twice as much energy as recycling it, so I tried to do my bit. Since the average person uses about 290 bags a year, that's a lot of wastage. I thought of making bags from the recycled fabric of my oldest clothes, but never got around to it, though I did use scraps of material as cleaning cloths.

So, armed with many handy tips, I set off to the shops with renewed vigour.

Exercise is good, and fresh foods are worth the extra effort, right? I would just have to make the time to shop for them and carry them home. I ate an awful lot of carrots and cabbages. I fell eagerly among dented cans of tomatoes or peaches or peas, which could be as little as 5p each. A little later in the year there would be apples and blackberries for the picking, and I resolved to fill the freezer up with those. If I had any fresh produce with bad bits in it, I just cut those out and ate the rest, instead of discarding the whole thing. Somehow I got 400g of fruit and veg. into myself every day, more or less, but all the other crap I was consuming was making me heavy. This was to be a year in protest against greed. Time to stop panicking about going hungry; it clearly wasn't a danger. As I sat sewing a button on my skirt, an inch further away from where it was before, I began to worry that I'd no longer fit my clothes, not in the way my friends had foreseen, but by getting too big for them all. That would be a disaster!

Bread and pastry products were never my staples before the year began. Now, however, I found loaves going for 10p before they dried out in the heat, and muffins and scones too. That kind of stuff was freezeable and light to carry, and suddenly I was getting through a hell of a lot of it. If I went into a coffee shop now, it was for a takeaway cup of hot water, and there was nothing at all, not even a biscuit, to buy for under a pound. No chance of cheating there, but what should have been a health bonus was going very wrong thanks to the excess left at the end of the day on supermarket bakery shelves.

In spite of Beverley's confident prediction, I hadn't turned into a vegetarian overnight: processed meat is not the thing to have hanging around in your supermarket past its sell-by date, so I got a lot of bargains in deli meats and ready meals, an hour before closing time. The trouble is, when you're tired from a long day's work and walking the last hour back home, the shopping weighs heavy on your arm. The sensible thing seems to be to eat some of your purchases on the way home.

Something had to be done about that. Either I could end the year as the fattest woman ever to survive on a pound a day, or I could take a look at my calories. Those chicken and mushroom pastries may be 5p each, but they're made of grease! Pork pies may seem a huge bargain when reduced by hundreds of percent, but there's nothing good about their ingredients. It's not like I work down a coal mine or something: teaching keeps you on your feet all day but it's mentally rather than physically arduous.

It broke my heart at first to see the bargains passing me by, and I became anxious about being far from home with no food and no money to buy any with, but of course there's always food. We can't get away from it. It's cheap and it's everywhere. So as long as I remembered to carry a few carrot sticks and nuts, or some cabbage-and-bean salad in my work bag, there was no need to fear.

One night in the city centre, I emerged from the pub. I'd been for a nice (free) soda water to catch up with a group of friends. I'd deliberately arrived late so they wouldn't notice my lack of money. Now it was nearly midnight, but the Tesco Metro was still open. Better check there in case there's anything going, I thought.

Outside, a cluster of street people were standing with their dogs, each holding a can of Special Brew. They were watching the assistants inside the shop as they wound everything up for the day. One of the lads drained his can and went inside in front of me, just as the assistant wheeled a trolley to the front. Last minute bargains! The Special Brew lad and I rifled through them as she piled them on the fridge shelves. Chilled pizzas 10p, pies 20p, cheesecake 25p. Nothing for me then. There was plenty to fill those lads up before they spent another night in the entrance to the multi-storey car park, though.

But the lad turned away again! We exchanged a look as we both went outside empty-handed.

'Nothing you fancy?' I asked. I could buy him a pie, even on my budget, if he wanted one.

'Nah, just seeing what there is. Ten minutes from now, that stuff's all in the wheelie by the car park. That's the time to get it.'

'You mean – dumpster diving?'

He laughed. 'If ya like, yeah. We get our scram out of there every night.'

It was tempting to hang around, just to see how they did it. It looked difficult, not to say dangerous, to get into one of those deep bins and rummage around in there for something half decent to eat. But if it had just been put in there minutes before, all wrapped up, surely it would be fine?

My feet were aching and I had to get up in the morning. I set off for home. It was silly to wait; there wasn't even anything I wanted. But I kept thinking about those lads and their way of playing the system. I'd Googled 'dumpster diving' after hearing about it on the radio, and found that for the 'Freegans' in the USA, it was a popular way of feeding themselves. They, their website announced, were an anti-consumerist group who saw no point in working just to get money, to say nothing of doing it to get rich. By not buying any goods from stores, Freegans believed they were boycotting an exploitative, destructive capitalist society. They survived on as little as possible, pooling their skills and resources and looking in restaurant and other bins and skips in the dead of night. The origins of their movement owed much to the hobos of the Depression era and the hippies of the sixties. These people, however, tended to be middle-class, well able to afford high quality foodstuffs, but they had made an ethical decision to live off waste. The consumerist lifestyle, they realised, was part of the world's problems, and something had to give.

Foraging trips in New York started around 9.30pm, after shops closed up and before the rubbish trucks arrived. The Freegans diligently re-tie bags after helping themselves, leaving everything just as it was before. The results of their forays are cooked up and shared out communally. They made much of the artificiality of sell-by dates, and the huge amount of food in America which is bought and then thrown out unused. Theirs was, I decided, a kind of a protest against throwing good food away in the first place. The New York Department of Sanitation estimates that £50 million of food are thrown away every year by local restaurants and business premises. I'm not sure how they worked that out, but it's a scary statistic even if it's only half true. New York has one in five people, including 118,000 children, suffering from hunger. To be honest, I found the British dumpster divers a bit scary too: they were very crusty-looking indeed, and the Freegans so passionate on the internet about their cause as to be a bit, well, evangelical.

The U.S. Department of Agriculture estimates that 27% of its production is wasted, while only one sixth of that amount was distributed to the world's 850 million starving people in 2004. In the British food chain, 17 million tonnes of waste is produced each year, a quarter still edible. Lettuce is top of the list: 61% of households throw one out every week.

Sell-by dates are scorned by the founder of www.freegan.info, Adam Weissman. He insists that the more upmarket the shop, the sooner the sell-by date. He reckons the product could still be edible for up to a fortnight after that. He says they are a bogus 'marketing strategy' and a 'culture of planned obsolescence' keeps us buying and wasting.

I was already using every scrap of everything I bought: I'd have soup for breakfast if it needed eating up. And therein lay another clue to my weight gain: the 'waste not want not' upbringing I'd endured was coming back to haunt me now my spending power was limited. In the 1940s, recycling and avoiding waste was a patriotic duty, but nowadays there are just too many leftovers for one woman to deal with. I felt suddenly sorry for all those fat single mums sitting around wolfing their kids' cold chips. And it does seem to me that it's women who are martyring themselves like that. It can be bad – if you make yourself eat what you don't need – or good if it's a way to feed yourself for free while saving the planet at the same time. Weissman says, 'Women are taught to keep compassion and co-operation at the centre of their value system, whereas men are more likely to buy into this competitive impulse that is the core of global capitalism.' Hence, Freeganism is spreading most rapidly among women in the 20-50 age range.

Well, it's a great way to save money, no doubt about that. But I couldn't help wondering what my students would say if they saw me raiding the bins; I think they'd assume I was underpaid. And I was by no means suffering from a lack of food these days. I didn't need to do it; it would surely make me fat. 'If I'm not hungry, it's wasted on *me!*' I repeated in my head, like a mantra, as I trudged home through the darkened streets of Bristol.

'Cantilever staircases? What are those?' Maunagh asked as she unpacked a coat from her bag and draped it over her shoulders. We were at the International Balloon Fiesta, sitting on a rug in a prime spot with a picnic, waiting for the 'Nightglow' to begin. As soon as it was dark, the huge collection of tethered balloons in front of us would light up the sky in time to music.

'I don't know actually. This is our opportunity to find out what they're all about,' I said, pouring tea from our flask.

It wasn't only supermarket bargains that kept me overfed: every day I still made time to go to the library, trawling the internet in search of free events in the area. These I listed meticulously in my diary, and if my friends wanted to socialise with me, they had to feign an interest in architecture or medicinal advances or whatever the lecturer chose to inflict upon them that evening. The university had a vast programme of public events. Their inaugural lectures were attended mostly by colleagues of the new professor, but members of the public were welcome. Furthermore, they were followed by a wine reception. Many an evening my dinner was nibbles and drinks, and I became a *connoisseuse* of the canapé. Medical students were the heaviest drinkers, I noted, while the geography faculty swept the buffet table like locusts. It wasn't only the food and drink which I enjoyed either: the speakers were usually very entertaining.

I learned about a lot about things I'd never come across before, including, well, cantilever staircases.

'I don't know what they are, but it said on the poster that there's coffee and biscuits from 5.15 and a reception afterwards, so I'm going to find out.'

'Will Ponytail be there?'

'He said he would. And the Nibbles Queen.'

We had nicknames for the half-dozen other regulars who attended the public lectures. To a man or woman, however, they had some kind of connection to the university, so my friends and I were the only genuine members of the public there. Nevertheless, everyone was unfailingly welcoming toward us, and when we staggered out of the reception rooms, replete, we'd always had a good time and met some very interesting people.

'What have you got for next Tuesday? I've got a lunchtime concert, with retiring collection,' said Maunagh.

Every few days we visited each other and compared diaries to see what free events we'd come across. My friends, sceptical as they had been to start with, were beginning to be won round to my latest idea of a good night out. All the people at the party who had shared their money troubles that night were finding that it was possible to go out with a pocketful of loose change, and come home drunk with their funds undamaged. We were learning all sorts of things and widening our social horizons too.

'Um, African art,' I said. 'First of a weekly series.'

'Lovely! I'll invite my art class,' she said. 'They were on about meeting for a drink somewhere, so we can kill two birds with one stone.'

'I'll ask Daphne. And I can wear my new jacket!'

'New to you, anyway. But that was quite a find. Do you ever come across anything that'd fit me?'

The Bristol kerbside collectors take clothes and shoes as well as newspapers and cans, and I had started scanning the recycling bins of the wealthier residents of Clifton on my way to and from work. This yielded some nice surprises, including a couple of items of clothing and a serviceable pair of sandals in my size, as well as plenty of the latest papers and magazines. I wasn't interested in the news, as I had the radio for that, but in the coupons and offers in between. In the *Bristol Evening Post,* there was a weekly free offer which could be claimed by collecting tokens every day. I took full advantage of thrown-out papers to get cinema tickets, lunches in a bakery or sandwich shop, admission to bowling or skating for myself and my friends, and even coffees for free one special day in Starbucks. What a treat! I hadn't realised how much my social life used to revolve around a cup of hot brown liquid consumed on a comfy chair with my cronies, or just by myself, watching the world go by. One of the hardest habits to break during my pound-a-day year was killing time over a coffee before an appointment somewhere, or easing into the weekend by planning a party in Coffee One. I wouldn't accept friends' offers to treat me; I would have nobody left by the end of the year at that rate. Instead we went to each other's houses, or out to the park or the waterfront with a flask, or a bottle and a couple of glasses.

I could still invite people out to the cinema with my coupons: some of us went to see *The Wind that Shakes the*

Barley at a multiplex preview; another time we gazed at Robert Redford in *An Unfinished Life*. Brand new films to talk about and nothing at all to pay – so far so good. I felt optimistic about my challenge, and although they all still thought I was insane, the people in my social circle were benefiting as well.

Eight o'clock on a Saturday morning. It was the day of the students' trip to Cambridge. It was still cold as I hurried up the hill to the school, puffing under the weight of my day-pack. It contained food and drink, defensive items against the British weather, a bottle of wine which had lost its label (reduced to 99p in Sainsbury's) and books. I'd found a second-hand shop with a box of giveaway items outside, and chosen several as gifts for Dan and Sarah. They were damned heavy though. I hoped they'd appreciate the gesture and not question why I'd invited myself for lunch in their garden rather than in one of the excellent restaurants in Cambridge.'

'It'll be lovely, eating al fresco in the summer. Do you mind?' I'd said in my email.

'Good idea, sis. We can move into the conservatory if it does rain.'

'I'll get myself there. Probably be with you at noon.'

The school bus was waiting, and a few of the more time-conscious students were too. I helped to check everyone in, put on a DVD, and enjoyed the cross-country journey much more than usual. When hitching it was expected I would chat to the driver, which is fine, but it doesn't leave time for gazing out of the window and watching the countryside passing by. It was only three months since I'd travelled by public transport at will, but I kind of missed the mindlessness of it. I was almost sorry to get off when we arrived, and start the hike to my brother's house.

'Nice to see you, sis!' Dan poured himself another glass of the plonk I had sneakily poured into a carafe while setting the table.

'What've you been up to this year? We haven't seen you for ages! Got any holidays booked?' asked Sarah. They had already told me about their plans to tour the Greek islands. Dan and his fiancée loved to spend money: the more you spent, the happier you were, in their philosophy.

'Well, I've been camping in Wales, and that was great. Really hot weather. And I had the campsite all to myself!' I replied truthfully.

'But aren't you going anywhere for a *proper* holiday? Sarah was pouring dressing onto a huge bowl of salad.

'Um – I'll just see if that bread's ready. Don't want it to burn.'

I escaped into the kitchen and retrieved my two 10p ciabattas from the oven. With 20p-worth of olives from the deli counter and a sprinkling of herbs and olive oil, they looked just fine.

Back in the garden, the conversation hadn't moved on very far. They were talking about their recently-purchased ruined farm cottage in Brittany. They were planning another trip to work on it while staying nearby. As we made our way through a divine Mediterranean fish soup, tearing off hunks of bread and passing salad and wine around, we chatted about the gastronomic delights of

France. The people in the village had been delightful to us on my previous visit there. I longed to go back and spend the days out of doors, working up an appetite for yet more fresh, simple food. Washed down with loads of wine, of course.

There in a sunlit English garden, the drink was beginning to have an effect. Yet again I felt a foolish impulse coming on.

'Would you like a hand doing that roof? I could probably come out and join you for a few days.'

'What a good idea!' enthused Sarah through a mouthful of salad.

'Great! We can put you up with us in the village. We've already sorted out a place,' added Dan.

I hadn't thought about the practicalities. Again. How could I get through a holiday in France without giving the game away? And how on earth was I going to get there in the first place, on a pound a day? If I managed to make the journey somehow, even if we were working and eating at the cottage, they'd want to go to the bar now and then. How was I going to pay my way?

But already they were taking up the idea and expanding on their plans.

'The neighbours could lend us an extra bike. We could all cycle down the canal path to the Sunday market.'

'We could go to that funny log cabin bar over there, on the way back.'

'I saw something about hiring horses, over at the campsite.'

'Hang on!' I cut in. 'I thought I was helping you fix the

roof? We can't go gadding about all over Brittany. Make the most of an extra pair of hands while I'm there.'

My brother put down his glass. 'We can work hard and play hard, sis. With the three of us we'll get everything done quicker!'

'You're probably right…' I quavered.

He mistook the reason for my hesitation. 'You won't hold us up. We could really do with your help. But we're all going out for a holiday as well, at the end of the day.'

'It'll be lovely!' said Sarah.

'We'll have a lot of fun,' I agreed. But at the back of my mind the disquiet was growing as I tried to imagine a holiday in France on a pound a day. Or would it be 1.4 Euros? That sounded like even less, somehow. And the challenge had to remain a secret…

What had I let myself in for now?

September

**I take drastic measures to save for a holiday, spend
nothing at all for a month, find some unusual ways
of making a few pounds for a rainy day, and
discover 'roadkill money'.**

Bern almost spat out his wine as he convulsed with
laughter. Coughing, he staggered to the open patio doors
and gasped for air. We could see his shoulders heaving from
where we stood at a high table arrayed with assorted snacks.
We were catching up with each other after a lecture on
obesity – a hot topic among my friends at the time.

Beverley gazed anxiously after him as she spoke. 'You
can't be serious! Tell me it's another of your jokes, for
goodness sake!'

'It's just impossible. You're going to come unstuck and
pack the whole thing in if you go to that extreme,' added
Maunagh.

'I've made up my mind. It's the only way to get a holiday
and make sure my brother doesn't notice what I'm up to,' I
insisted. 'And I've reserved a pound for cash collections at
work. I've already started.'

Bern was returning with a bottle of wine. His cheeks
were flushed and his eyes watered.

'Tell me I misheard that, please,' he said, refilling all our
glasses.

'You got it right,' said Bev. 'She isn't spending any money
at all now!'

I'd racked my brains on the bus back from Cambridge. How on earth could I go to France on holiday at the end of September? I'd need some spending money, clearly. And something in reserve in case of a dire emergency, like an accident or a robbery. I could hitch, and find free places to camp, and carry food. There were even opportunities for free travel on the ferries with continental lorry drivers, who automatically received a ticket for two people. But once I arrived, Dan and Sarah mustn't guess what I was living on, so I'd need a bit of money in reserve. There was nothing else for it: I had to stop spending altogether, and save up thirty-four of my pounds, to take with me. And if I could think of any other (legal) ways of coming by money without working for it, I'd try to amass a stash of reserve cash, and carry that just in case.

Bern waved an arm at the beautiful view of Clifton beyond the balcony. 'Everybody would be doing that if it was possible!' he said. 'You're mad!'

'It's only for a month. I've got loads of stuff stocked up at home, and I can keep going to events like tonight's for my dinner and social life. By the way, does anyone want to come to the Kite Festival at Ashton Court this weekend? There's lots of entertainment and the weather looks good.'

We were certainly not going short of food or drink. The public lecture season was in full swing and there were buffet receptions like this on a regular basis.

'Isn't it illegal to go around without any money on you? I thought I read that somewhere,' asked Heather.

'There is some state in America where you could get arrested if you're not carrying sufficient funds. It's to stop

47

beggars, I think. But I don't think the same thing happens here,' I said, sipping my wine.

'You're not taking up begging next, are you?' asked Bev, reaching for more complimentary rocket salad.

'No, but if I see a coin on the street, I'll pick it up and save it in my emergency fund.'

Recently, I'd been coming across loose change all over the place. Scouring the streets had become hard-wired into the miles I walked every day, and on the way to the lecture, almost without thinking, I'd picked up a 20p piece winking at me from the gutter. But where do you stop? I've lifted up the sofa cushions in my favourite coffee shop (having dropped my pen) and found a veritable nest of litter: tissues and fluff and sugar packets and, yes, coins, sitting unloved and unsought week after week. The staff don't overdo their cleaning at the end of the day, clearly. Don't blame them. It's a long day on your feet, but it did cross my mind that it might be worth their while to brush down the soft furnishings once in a while. Well, I would happily give them a hand if I was ever short of a few bob. What was the legal position on picking up small change, though? The police would laugh in your face if you handed it in. The shop staff would probably pocket it. And when did you start reporting money you'd found? If it was a quid? A fiver? Twenty?

The *Daily Mail*, ever ready with little-known facts to amaze the nation, printed an article about 'the great lost tribe of penny pieces' which nobody bothers to pick up. They estimate that sofas across the nation contain £5.9 million pounds' worth of pennies, drains £650,000, and the streets, mind-bogglingly, may hold £26 million of dropped pennies.

They quoted the Royal Mint, which says £61.5 million's worth of penny coins have gone missing from circulation since they were introduced in 1971. That's a pound for each person in the country! Those mislaid coins would together weigh as much as a Royal Navy battleship, they added. Furthermore, the metal in a penny is actually worth 1.65p. And those figures only took into account our smallest coin; I regularly picked up coins of other denominations, and notes too. I remembered the old saying: 'Look after the pennies and the pounds will look after themselves.' With that in mind, I resolved to pick up everything I found and add it to my precious stash of emergency holiday money.

The first drop of water made it past my collar and down my neck. I couldn't do anything about it. I was pushing my bike up the pavement, slogging towards the top of Park Street. Umbrellas jostled in the Friday night bustle. Again and again I swerved when someone stopped in their tracks, lured by the siren call of something in a shop window. The lights, the warmth, the abundance inside contrasted sharply with the unseasonal grimness of the evening. Selfishness was palpable on the streets as people coveted, planned for the weekend, struggled for home.

Fine gritty spray lashed the side of my face as a van sped downhill, far too fast. At the same time a cluster of wet carrier bags hit me behind the knee and their owner tutted at me as if I alone was to blame for the weather, the burgeoning dusk, her lateness.

I had no carrier bags over my handlebars. There was no need for me to hurry except to get out of the rain. In spite of my discomfort it was good to feel distanced from all that frantic activity, in my own little bubble on the street. I just hoped it wouldn't be this rainy when I was camping in France.

A beggar called to me from a doorway, probably because I was the only one whose eyes were not taken by the shops. I smiled at him but carried on, getting in the way, creating with my bike another unwelcome presence in the commercial district. He probably did well while people were out to spend, loose change weighing too heavy in their pockets. His expression was the same as the shoppers': half hopeful, half resigned.

I concentrated on the acute angle of the flagstones ahead. Gobbets of saliva shone in the rain like baby jellyfish among the sweet wrappers and trampled discs of chewing gum. I wouldn't like to be sitting on that pavement with the beggar. I was following behind the boots of a couple of young girls clip-clopping up the hill. Sodden fur and pompoms at the backs swung jauntily over the muck. I concentrated on those four feet which crossed and recrossed in front of me as the girls were distracted by this and that in the shops. I toiled along behind like Good King Wenceslas's page.

One of the boots came down on a pinkish bit of litter, almost tearing it, but on they went. I, however, stopped. The piece of paper was sodden and plastered to the street. I peeled it off the flagstones. It was a twenty-pound note. Someone who hadn't been paying attention bumped into the back wheel of my bike, swore at me and swept on. The note dripped in my hand, an unpleasant thing to hold. Filthy lucre, I thought.

Another pedestrian made a show of getting past, so I started walking again with the money crushed into my handlebar as I pushed the bike. I didn't know what to do. Should I go back and give the beggar the chance to buy a fun-sized rock of crack? That didn't seem right. Give it to the police? A lot of hassle for them and for me; I didn't think they'd thank me for my efforts. Well, one thing was for sure: I wouldn't spend it.

What do you do with an extra twenty quid when you've pledged to live on a pound a day for a year? I didn't have the answer. For now I'd put it with the rest: the other two twenties, two tenners and a two-pound coin, all of which I'd found on the street since June. Plus a Tupperware box full of small change, all of which I hoped to convert into notes to secrete in a money-belt for my trip to France.

When I talked about the 'roadkill money' I was finding everywhere, my friends were amazed, and in some cases frankly disbelieving. It was as shocking to them that money was lying around under their noses as it was that I had been getting by on so little for the last three months. They were jealous although they would never dream of trying my challenge themselves. I watched a series of emotions flash across the face of each person as we talked about it: 'I don't believe you!' 'You're mad!' 'You must be depriving someone else, someone like me, in order to do this!' and ultimately, 'What would I do with all the money you must be saving?'

This month without spending anything at all was a different kind of a challenge. I had plenty of supplies left in my room to keep me going until I returned from France, and without the dubious excitement of scouring the shops for bargains, I had a lot more time on my hands. I read books. I got life-coaching from Lilli, who was not yet at her wits' end. I created exciting packed lunches from my kitchen cupboard. And luckily, because it had been a hot summer, there was a great deal of fruit to be scrumped. I went black-berrying and collected hazelnuts, beating the squirrels at their own game. It was, sadly, a bad year for sweet chestnuts, which brought back fond memories of childhood trips, nutting in the woods. I was too afraid of poisoning myself to pick mushrooms, except for the beautiful puffballs, which couldn't possibly be mistaken for anything else. The danger of lead poisoning from petrol fumes on the roadside fruit I collected seemed less to me than that of picking stuff low down on the bushes, where dogs had peed. I got loads of apples, plums too, from hedgerow trees standing where once there were orchards, when new roads were created in north Bristol.

I read about collecting hawthorn berries and nettles, wood sorrel and rosehips, but these all needed expensive additional ingredients to make them palatable. Foraging around the edge of fields after mechanical harvesters had been through was suggested by one publication, but I was never in the right place at the right time. As for maize, in England it isn't usually the delectable sweetcorn you might expect, but dry stuff used for cattle food. So I didn't go trespassing on farmers' land, but gathered from the abundant supplies on the wayside.

I cycled hundreds of miles, loading the panniers with food for free. Every day, it seemed, I came across another idea to help me live well without spending money.

But I couldn't have done it without a little help from my friends.

The umpteenth little dog ran up to me and started barking from a safe distance. Its owner called it half-heartedly from across the park. My feet were soggy and my arm was aching from sweeping my new toy across the wet grass. Should have worn wellies, of course.

Beep! The metal detector's display pointed to '25c.' Unlikely in the West Country, perhaps, but no less desirable for that. Who was to say that some American tourist hadn't travelled across one of the flyovers above me? They would surely have been driven wild and reckless by the spectacular view: the garden centre and bonded warehouses bordering the coffee-coloured river Avon. 'Wow, Marlene, this sure is quaint! Look at those cute kids making mud pies down there in the park. Let's give 'em somethin' to dig fer!'

And with that perhaps they flung a handful of change out of an open-topped Cadillac into the grass below.

I scuffed with my heel at the spot the detector had indicated. Nothing to be seen. But wait – here was the edge of a shiny disc... The detector beeped again, this time pointing to a picture of bottle tops and nails. Right. Another bottle top. There was certainly a lot of litter in the grass, when you got up close and personal. A hell of a lot of dog dirt as well. But so far, nothing in the way of diamond rings or pound coins or even lost keys.

That was why my friends Philippe and Linda had bought the detector in the first place: they'd dropped their car keys on a golf course. Because of the car's complicated burglar-proof electronic lock, it was going to cost them a fortune to replace them. But the detector hadn't come up trumps for them either.

'Found anything yet?' A portly fellow with a walking stick had been watching me; I wondered for how long.

'Nothing, but I don't really know what I'm doing. I've never tried this before.'

'Well, if you don't mind me saying so, you need to hold it a bit lower. Don't skim the grass, iron it!'

'Iron it?'

'Yes, like this,' he demonstrated with his stick. 'But watch out for the parkie!'

'It's not illegal, is it?' I was alarmed at the prospect of a fine. No wonder the dogs didn't like me. They know a criminal when they see one.

'Oh, no. You can use a detector, but you can't dig.'

'Well, that's fine. I'm not digging.'

'Just say you've lost yer ring. We used to have a lot of fun with one of those when I was young.'

He chatted nostalgically about the highlights of his metal-detecting career. Myself, I was doing it just to see what there was, after reading that *Daily Mail* article about the lost millions of coins in Britain. I had been lent the detector as soon as I started my year, but I hadn't got around to using it until this month of not spending at all.

I got some tips on using the detector, then he left me to discover such important archaeological finds as flattened cans, ring pulls and more bottle tops. The wind was whistling around the pillars of the road above and the traffic noise was starting to get on my nerves. I had soon had enough.

I switched off the machine and removed the batteries as the man with the stick had instructed, and headed for home. I'd have to find a better place to search. The beach, perhaps. Nobody could stop you digging on the beach, could they?

The detector was beginning to get heavy. I paused for a moment to change it over to my other arm, and noticed something shiny on the pavement. After two hours of metal detecting, all I had to show for it was a 10p piece, picked up on the corner of my own street.

My backpack stood half-full in my room, open to receive extra items for my trip as they crossed my mind. I had just added a map from the library, a penlight torch and eight white T-shirts printed with the word CREW on the back, which I'd found in a bag beside an over-full clothes recycling bin. The printing had smeared slightly, so they had been thrown out, brand new. Useful for the three of us in France, I thought, since laundry would be hard to do where we were staying.

I moved on to my next job, the hoovering. The messy part came first: taking out the bag and emptying it of its contents. Better than buying new bags though! After a fit of sneezing, the job was done. Just three days to go now before my trip, and I was counting down what was left to do: pack some portable food, choose a couple of books, and work out a route. I'd posted ads on the ride-sharing websites but there was nobody going at the right time except for one bloke in a van. He seemed to specialise in taking prospective hitchers and charging them more than the bus fare for the privilege of sharing a journey he was doing anyway. I could do without his help. I wanted to go straight from work on Thursday, cross the Channel at Dover overnight, and keep on going west from Calais as the sun came up. With luck, after a full day's hitching on the Friday, I'd be able to camp near to where my brother was staying, and arrive fresh and ready to do some work on the Saturday. I made a trip to the fridge and came back with my dinner: summer pudding. I had been glad of my frozen bread reserves over the month. My housemates had not commented on the contents of my section of the freezer, but since keeping the appliance full uses less electricity, I felt I was doing them a favour.

On my journey I would take sandwiches as well as apples and dried apple chips. I'd even made a couple of pots of jam for us to have with our croissants before we started our demolition work in the mornings. This final week, my dinners consisted mainly of fruit crumbles and things on toast. I'd been lucky too that one of my colleagues had been house-sitting for a friend who kept hens and a large kitchen garden. I went over one evening to help her pick the beans, and came back with bags full of fresh vegetables and eggs. It would have been a more monotonous month without such bonuses from people I knew.

I took out the map and pored over it while eating. I wanted to stay on the busiest roads, and not stray too far off when finding a place to camp. It would be easy to get stuck in the countryside early on a Saturday morning if I was too far off the beaten track. But the thing about hitching, of course, is that you can never tell where you'll end up: that's the most exciting thing about it. And when you speak French as badly as I do, anything could happen!

It was already 9pm. I had agreed not to eat anything after that time because of a psychology experiment I was doing the next day, so I put away the remains of my dinner. University research students, I had found, put up notices on campus advertising for volunteers for their experiments. Some involved testing drugs, others got people to sit at a computer and go through a series of tasks. They often paid a few pounds for the volunteers' trouble, and over the month I'd been a guinea-pig for several people, building my emergency fund without withdrawing anything from the bank. I'd rated faces according to how attractive I found them. I'd listened to words on a recording and tried to recall as many as possible, or matched and organised pictures and descriptions on a computer, all of which was quite fun to do. The task for the next day, however, suited me even better: I was to get all my meals for free!

I got up an hour early and arrived sleepily at the psychology lab. An equally tired-looking PhD student, Henk, handed me a bunch of questionnaires and disclaimers. It was hard to concentrate when I hadn't even had a cup of tea that morning, but I waded through the forms as various other volunteers drifted in. At last we were all taken to separate booths, and from a hatch in the back, our breakfast arrived. First, we had to finish a really thick, heavy yoghurt drink, which was the point of the test. Henk was working on appetite and its suppression and that gloopy drink was the key. After that, we could eat as much as we wanted. The amount we got through was carefully weighed and recorded, and the process repeated at lunch and dinner time. In between, I went to work as normal, feeling uncomfortably full but otherwise rather smug and virtuous. Another day without spending any money; another day closer to my holiday. It seemed less impossible now to survive in France without giving away my secret. I was beginning to look forward to the adventure.

October

I relate the tale of my French adventure and how generous people can be, find a coach trip even I can afford, learn about liberated books and blow £7 in the Big Smoke.

'The tablecloth's blowing away!' giggled Heather.

'Grab the cups, quick!' cried Daphne, clasping hers and Martin's to her bosom.

A paper plate of crisps upended its contents onto the dangerously billowing tablecloth. Unfazed, Bern began to eat them while still keeping his other hand on the stack of recycled plastic cups (from my work's vending machine) and watching Lewis and Finn, Helen and Neil's children. They were tremendously excited by our windy waterfront picnic, and crowed with rosy-faced glee every time something blew over.

We were celebrating my return from France. Everybody was dying to know how I'd got on, so I'd organised a picnic on one of the tables at the harbourside, to tell them all about it. Unfortunately, the weather was proving something of a distraction.

At last everything was under control, as long as we clasped our cups and our food in our hands, and rather impolitely kept our elbows firmly on the table. The sun was shining but it wasn't having much effect. Heather had her hood up and Maunagh had tucked herself into a car rug like an invalid on a seaside rest cure.

I had brought back some token items from France: some extremely rough red wine in tetra-brick boxes and some jars of paté, both from a Calais hypermarket. I'd also made flasks of soup to have with bread or crackers. In spite of what I'd said, the others had brought things too, so there was plenty to blow into the harbour if the wind got gusty again.

'A toast!' called Daphne, raising her cup. 'The wanderer's return!'

As we tapped our plastic cups together Lewis and Finn could be heard demanding a piece of toast too.

'Come on, then,' said Maunagh, 'tell us how it went, before we all freeze!'

I grinned. 'I was very lucky really. I got straight onto the M4 after work, and even after dark I found good places to get lifts.'

'Didn't you have loads of luggage, though?' asked Helen. 'I can't believe you brought stuff back!'

'It wasn't too bad. My tent and sleeping bag are tiny, and some of the stuff I took out there was to use up or give away. And I took old work-clothes and didn't bring them back.'

'I couldn't walk with a big backpack, though,' said Daphne. 'Not these days.'

'Well, I didn't have to walk much at all,' I said. 'Most of the time it was just from one car to another.'

On the south side of the M25, I had asked the driver of the car I was in to drop me at Clacket Lane Services, although he was going a few miles further. I knew this was a good place to get a lift onto a ferry: a lot of the continental drivers stopped there for a break before tackling the last stretch of their drive down to the docks. I sat in the coffee bar with a cup of hot water and one of my many sandwiches, and optimistically wrote out a sign that said FRANCE. I was wearing my lucky hitch-hiking shirt, white with pink and mauve candy stripes. It always looked clean (even when it was dirty), stood out against the tarmac, and characterised me as female, cheerful and harmless from a hundred metres' distance.

'You are going to France?' A well-dressed woman had paused by my table, takeaway cup in hand.

'Yes, I'm hitch-hiking,' I said, although it must have been obvious as I sat there beside my backpack.

'I can take you zere. I am French.'

And so it was that Helene put my luggage in the boot of her car and took me through the Tunnel, saving me a long and tiring night on the cross-channel ferry. And it was all paid for already by her company, which regularly sent employees to and fro. The only trouble was that instead of getting to Calais at dawn, I arrived at one in the morning with no chance of getting another lift. The ferry had the advantage of a lorry drivers' canteen where I could have asked if anyone was going westward off the boat, but on the train we just dozed and chatted in the car. We discussed how poorer regions were more accepting of hitchers, since cars are more of a luxury. She agreed that the mobile phone was a huge asset to the safety of a hitcher, as well as a boon to females driving alone. Helene used to hitch herself, and now looked out for people to help out in return, although in Britain she had only come across the 'trade plate drivers' who had been delivering a car. They brandish their registration plates as an indication of their profession and a mark of their legitimacy. I'd never seen one of those guys hang around for very long: other people driving for a living would pick them up in no time.

Helene was very helpful. She was on her way to visit her parents just outside the port, but she knew of a campsite on the road I wanted, and offered to drop me there, even though it was dark and late and she was as tired as I was. We had both been working all day and travelling all evening, after all. In spite of this, she cheerfully dropped me at the campsite gates and planted kisses on both of my cheeks before speeding off into the night.

In the sudden silence, I looked around. There wasn't a single tent to be seen, just a few caravans on the muddy grass, all in darkness. Stealthily, I skirted the perimeter hedge, hoping there were no dogs to start barking. Just behind the campsite, I spread my tent out on the soggy ground. With my sleeping bag inside it, it was like a survival bag. I was asleep in moments.

My eyes snapped open to grey daylight. It was six in the morning and time to get going. I packed my bag, left it hidden in the hedge, and crept through to the camp ground's ablutions block. The showers were cold but did the job of freshening me up for the day.

People were kind as I made my way towards Brittany, lift by short-distance lift. Some tried to practise their English, others offered to share their food. It was a long way, but I headed inexorably westward, finally calling it a day at Dol-de-Bretagne. The town was delightful and the sun was shining. I sat in the square to have a picnic. Also in my bag were three postcards of Brittany, bought in a Bristol charity shop for 1p each. They had survived without becoming too dog-eared. I wrote one to my father, another to my colleagues and a third to Maunagh, who would pass on word of my progress.

'So far, so good – meeting brother tomorrow. About to spend first Euros – on stamps!' I wrote, and posted the cards before heading out to a sheltered copse where I camped snug and dry.

'So were they expecting you on the Saturday morning?' asked Heather. We had either got used to the chilly wind or developed an inner glow thanks to the wine and soup.

'I'd emailed before they left to say I'd try to be there for eight in the morning, just before they started work. And it was *exactly* eight when I spotted my brother loading up his car, and got my driver to hoot at him. He was gobsmacked!'

Luck was on my side the whole time I was there. The weather was balmy, so it was easy to get Dan and Sarah to agree to home-cooked dinners in the back garden. We replaced broken roof tiles, treated wormy beams and bashed plaster from the old stone walls. We picnicked among the rubble at lunchtime and sat together preparing fresh food at night. We were staying in an apartment lent by friends of theirs, which was much better than camping. Sarah took some hilarious photos of us in our 'crew' T-shirts, and it was heart-warming to see the two of them so much in love. No doubt that worked in my favour, too, as they were more oblivious to the material world than they normally would have been.

'But what about the *money?*' Maunagh asked. 'Didn't they notice?'

'It was a good job they're so smitten with each other, or they might have wondered why we had to have candlelit suppers *á maison!*' I laughed. 'And I slipped away to the big supermarket the first evening I was there, and came back with lots of bargains. We come from a family who don't waste food, so we had to use everything up!'

'You must have gone out, though, surely,' said Neil, taking a wriggling Finn on his knee. 'Did you buy rounds?'

'Yes, we had a bike ride or a walk every evening, calling at a bar on the way. But we'd only have one or two drinks, then make up for that with wine at home over dinner.'

'So you stayed within your budget?' asked Helen, passing round a bag of Bombay mix.

'Even though we had a really lovely, busy time, and had a great laugh, and lived very well, I spent less than I'd saved up for the trip. You know, I completely forgot that I still had another pound a day for every day I was there, as well as what I'd put aside. And the journey back was all free too! That's why I had to use up my spare Euros and buy food in Calais.'

It was sad to say goodbye on the outskirts of town, the morning I left. It was still pleasant weather, as it had been for the whole of the four days I'd spent in Brittany. I held up my sign, and as is often the way in little towns, the first car to approach stopped to give me a lift. Dan and Sarah, who were waiting across the road to see me off, were highly amused by this, and waved enthusiastically as we sped away.

Once again the lifts were short but I was promptly picked up again each time I put out my thumb. People often went out of their way to drop me at a good spot such as a service station or a busier on-ramp on the *autoroute*. Just as in England, the drivers were from all walks of life. Some picked me up to help themselves to stay awake, some felt sorry for me, others needed someone to keep their kids amused, or wanted to moan to me about the tribulations of their job. But as evening approached, the traffic thinned considerably. When a woman in an open sports car left me at the *pèage* near her house, there was hardly a soul to be seen.

'Most of the trucks are going to stop for the night now. There is not much traffic during the night here,' she told me, handing me a business card. 'If nobody takes you on, call us and you can sleep at our house.'

How very generous, I thought, as she helped me with my luggage and clasped my hands in goodbye. I must send her an email once I'm back.

I never guessed that an hour later I'd still be standing by the *peage*. The only lorries going through were obviously very local, and car drivers gave me a regretful shrug or pointed to the left or right: they were turning off the road soon. I took out the card and turned it over and over in my hand. Then I shouldered my pack and crossed the road, to hitch into town.

The Delafosse family were delightful. When I called from a bar on the main street, Marianne came straight out to collect me. I was introduced to her husband, who was cooking dinner, her three lanky teenage sons and their

65

'surprise' blonde-haired baby girl. The boys had all done exchange holidays in England but were understandably bashful about conversing over dinner with an English teacher. They disappeared as soon as was politely possible afterwards, scurrying around upstairs. I later found that they had been detailed to prepare one of the boys' rooms for me, and that unlucky sibling had to share a room for the night. I was very touched by their efforts, and even more so when Marianne excused herself to make a phone call. When she returned, she announced that she would be travelling towards Calais in the morning with the baby, to visit her mum. So, guess what – she could give me a lift!

I was overwhelmed by their generosity. The whole family had made sacrifices for a complete stranger. I would have been happy to roll out my sleeping bag in the lounge and creep out at daybreak back to the motorway, but they had really done their best for me. It was only in the car the next day that Marianne explained their philosophy. Their eldest son had been in a horrific car crash the year before, and would have died had it not been for passers-by who stopped to help. Since then, they all had vowed to help anyone they could, whenever and wherever possible, because they were so grateful to those strangers who had saved their boy's life.

'It is easy – we have a lot. And nobody knows how much longer their life will be,' said Marianne, her eyes filling with tears as she recalled that terrible time.

The surprise baby in the back slept soundly all the way, so we had time to reflect on what she had said. And I wholeheartedly agreed with her: we all have enough to give something away.

The service station where Marianne dropped me was just perfect. The car park was full of lorries, many from the U.K., so I just asked around at the filling station and in no time was the 'co-driver' of an Englishman going to Northampton. Not the right direction for me on the other side, but he was confident that one of the other drivers on the boat would be able to take me towards the M4 and home. It was quite a leisurely day: browsing in the hypermarket, having coffee brewed on a primus stove in the ferry car park while waiting for the boat, eating a free roast dinner in the drivers' canteen before we had even set sail, and chatting to the other drivers on our table. As predicted, someone offered to take me to Swindon as soon as they found out I was hitching. We met outside the duty-free shop when the first call sounded to say arrival was imminent, and I swapped my bag from one cab to the other down in the bowels of the boat. That was that: I was home the same night after a very exciting week away.

'You've got some balls, though!' said Helen.

'Yes, I'm not brave enough to do all that, just going up to people at the petrol station and asking for a lift. What if they said no?' asked Heather.

'If they say no, you just ask someone else. I used to hitch with my daughter when she was small, back in the Seventies,' said Maunagh.

All eyes swivelled to her. 'You hitch-hiked with a baby?' asked Daphne.

'Everybody hitched in those days. It's become more rare since then, more suspicious. But there's still enough nice people to make it worthwhile,' I put in.

'We were fine. But I wouldn't do it now,' Maunagh went on. 'Too many mad people out there.'

Neil was laughing. 'Anyone looking at us now would think we were all bloody barking,' he said.

We looked around at our chaotic table. It was threatening to rain. We were all bundled up with just a small space left between hood and scarf to introduce food into our mouths. We looked like refugees resting on the march. It was a full-time job holding onto the wildly flapping tablecloth, which was covered in the remains of our picnic.

'Whose idea was this, anyway?' laughed Daphne, blowing on her frozen fingers.

We were all giggling as we started packing everything away.

I could hardly believe it was true. I clicked on 'Go to checkout' and the computer screen gave me my total bill: £1.50! At last I had found a bus cheap enough for me to afford, and it was going all the way from London to Bristol. Megabus was only a pound per journey, plus the 50p booking fee, so I was planning a weekend away to use up the seven extra pounds accumulated unspent while I was away in France. It would be easy to hitch in to London, but it was hard to get out to the fringes of the Big Smoke to come back. The bus, from Victoria, would make it very easy. I hadn't been on any public transport for months! I smiled as I keyed in my cashcard details. It suddenly seemed like the height of luxury, sitting in an old double-decker for almost three hours. Once my place was reserved and I'd noted the booking number, I surfed a few sites for free events in London. Lots of things going on! I made some notes after checking the locations in my borrowed London A–Z. Daphne was letting me stay in her flat in the Barbican, on a rare weekend when nobody was in it. It would be lovely, in the anticlimactic late autumn days after my holiday, to go somewhere again.

This time, as I stood at Gordano Services, my luggage was even smaller. It was Friday afternoon and I was wearing plenty of warm stuff. Most importantly, I had my old trainers on. They were going to cover a lot of miles with me, since the Underground and buses were out of the question. The A–Z was vital too, along with the ubiquitous pack of sandwiches and a flask of black tea. My only other book, a novel, wasn't coming back with me: I'd recently discovered Bookcrossing.

On a bench in Ashton Court, on a windy bike ride, I'd noticed a package wrapped in a plastic bag. It was still there when I came back, and curiosity overcame me. I picked it up, unwrapped a book, and opened it to discover a message on a slip of paper. 'To the finder of this book – congratulations! I hope you enjoy it as much as I did! J.'

It was a liberated book, left there by someone who had read it and passed it on, having perhaps found it lying around somewhere before. The Bookcrossing website even allows you to track your books: if you put an ID number inside, the finder can log on and tell you where they found and left it. You can buy labels and stickers for your books, too, but that isn't obligatory. For me, it was even handier than the library, and my Bristol book was going to move a hundred miles or so up the M4 with me, for some lucky Londoner to find.

It was a good time to be travelling. Lots of people had knocked off work early, like me, and were putting their weekend plans into action. A gay couple, going up for a weekend of clubbing, dropped me near the London Eye, and I set off happily along the Embankment. The river looked magical with the city lights reflected in its surface. People hurried by on their way to who knew where, but I had plenty of time to appreciate the world-famous sights for free. Yet again I was struck by the thought that if we all worked less, the time would outweigh the lack of money. A driver who had picked me up on the way had made me think. He was a self-employed decorator, and he had worked out that he'd be able to have a day off every week, if it wasn't for the expense of running his vehicle.

'But I can't do without it!' he'd said.

In vain I'd tried to discuss ways he could downsize his life: his wife had a car, and was at home with their kids most of the time. He could have more time with the family if only they could work something out between them. Most of the work he did was local, and once he'd dropped off the equipment for a job, he'd be able to walk or cycle to home and back. Was a car so essential that you had to spend a fifth of your working week supporting its cost?

It was the same with other people who complained about their crippling mortgages and bills. They seemed to accept their lot as inevitable, without a thought of how much more freedom they could have simply by living a little more lightly. My thoughts turned back to Marianne. Nobody knows what might hit them tomorrow. Better to enjoy today, while it's here.

Covent Garden was abuzz with activity. I lingered a while, eating my supper and watching the buskers and fire-eaters and magicians. They seemed to be doing pretty well in tips from the crowd, I thought, as I added a few coppers to a hat. Perhaps I could do some busking if things got a bit tight!

At last I found the flats and went up in the warmth of the lift. I had a long list of things to see and do that weekend: galleries, free concerts, a book launch and a couple of events in museums. I had been tipped off about flash-mobbing too: the underground organisers give e-bulletins to people who subscribe to their website, then confirm the venue for a crazy live event a few hours before it kicks off. And didn't it kick off! They organised a pillow fight in Trafalgar Square, and an iPod 'silent rave' where a huge crowd suddenly threw down their coats and bags and started dancing to the music in their headphones. That was something I'd love to see. I wasn't going to miss out on culture either: the Royal Court Theatre in Sloane Square had an offer I could hardly believe. An hour before their shows, they offered restricted view seating for 10p per person! How could I resist! As I snuggled in to the cosiness of my bed, I wondered if there would be an opportunity to spend any money at all.

'Perhaps I could go down to 50p a day,' I thought as sleep overtook me.

November

Organising a clothes swap, finding ways to pass the long dark evenings and things to do for free.

I had just dipped my sleeve in the palette again.

'If you have the paint a bit thicker on your brush, you'll have more control over where it goes. And you can add some interesting texture as well,' said Katie, looking over my shoulder.

It was my first attempt at oil painting. I'd enjoyed art at school, but had done almost nothing since then, although I love galleries. Recently, Heather and I had been to the opening night of a students' art exhibition at a school on the fringes of town. The atmosphere had been very festive, especially since the budget had run to a buffet and drinks. More interesting still, there had been a poster in the hall advertising free art classes for adults and children alike, running weekly through the autumn term. I was told that it was an attempt to get the wider community interested, since they had until recently been struggling to provide a decent education for people from the vast housing estates nearby. Now extra money had been provided and incentives such as cash bonuses for exam passes were being offered, in radical attempts to save a failing school. Well, this member of the community was more than willing to spread the word and learn to paint in the dark evenings heralding the end of the year.

It was such a pity so few people had signed up: the

teacher, a recent arts graduate, was so keen and so nice, and the school had provided very generously for us. There were free hot drinks, all art materials provided, and the radio playing softly in the background as we laboured over our canvases in the studio.

'Who's that going to be for?' I asked the only child in the group.

'If it's any good, I'll give it to my dad. Or my gran.' He had copied a scene from a car ad in a magazine: a four-wheel drive in a desert sunset. It was really very good, and I said so.

'He shows me up!' laughed his mum, coming in with her coffee and a handful of biscuits. She had started and re-started a painting from a photograph of the family in Tenerife. There were only four more classes, and I was beginning to wonder if she'd have anything to show at the end. But at least her son was having a great time.

I turned back to my still life. It wasn't good at all, but I was stubborn enough to keep on with it. Perhaps I'd learn something in the process.

There were only three other people in our group: a retired couple and a woman who worked as a classroom assistant part-time. If Katie was disappointed with the turnout, she didn't say so. And for those of us who had come along, it meant more individual help.

On the way home, I diverted to the Suspension Bridge again. It was November 5th, and quite warm. I wheeled my bicycle to the wider part of the viewpoint at the foot of the bridge chains, and looked down over the city. I could see my little shabby street with four lanes of traffic pouring past, far below, and the odd flurry of light as someone let off a firework in one of the back gardens. In Long Ashton a big display was going on, and from my vantage point I saw it all, lighting up the night sky in a cascade of pyrotechnic splendour. It was all mine for the watching. I felt a sudden surge of love for where I lived and the life I took part in there. Bristol had so much to offer, was so good to me. I couldn't imagine having so much fun, on so little money, anywhere else in the world.

I had found lots of regular events to go to as the evenings darkened into winter. There was the series of autumn architecture lectures at the university, or free meditation classes at the local community centre. In meditation, I found myself a bit of a fidget, though, and ten minutes of staring at a candle flame I find is usually enough at one sitting. Then there was my book club. I'd been going there for a long time, meeting in a church hall. It was surprising how often I stumbled upon great books I would normally never have considered reading. Even if the book was not to my taste, there was still plenty to talk about. I usually got copies from the library, or if they were new ones, I read them over four or five visits to my favourite bookshops, which provided comfy chairs for the purpose of browsing. The monthly contribution to the room the club hired was £1, but by happy coincidence in my year of living on a pound a day, God had spoken to the church committee that spring and told them to waive the fees of their room rentals, to encourage people into the fold.

It was nice to have a day out for free from time to time too. My local branch of the British Trust of Conservation

Volunteers takes a minibus full of people out most days to help on conservation projects. There was no need to book: you just had to turn up with a packed lunch at ten in the morning, wearing your oldest clothes. That autumn I was enjoying some wonderful times in places I wouldn't otherwise have been able to go to. I cleared brambles on a vast estate among shaggy Highland cattle. I learned dry stone walling amid wonderful views on Dundry hill. And later in the year I was to have a go at hedge-laying. We were a mixed bag of volunteers: some retired, some out of work, others with learning difficulties. I spoke to people I wouldn't otherwise have met, and got their take on life. It was always worth going. There was invariably an expert to watch over us, making sure we were using tools safely, and cheerfully answering our questions. The work was punctuated by frequent breaks for coffee and biscuits. If the weather was bad, we packed up early, but generally we were driven home by four o'clock, pleasantly tired and muddy. I had done residential volunteering before for the National Trust, but the £75 or so they asked as a contribution for board and lodging was out of the question this year. Still, if any other such opportunities came up, I was on the lookout for them.

It was getting easier to choose my 'oldest' clothes for working out of doors: lots of my things were looking distinctly shabby. I still kept a few half-decent things aside for work, ironing my blouses nicely as I'd promised Lilli. From time to time I got a free make-up demonstration in a department store or a 'makeover' in branches of the Body Shop. These, and my hairdressers' modelling sessions, kept me respectable enough. But I had to confess I was getting a bit bored with my weekend wardrobe. I hadn't bought anything new to wear for six months, and I fancied a change.

'But what about big people, like Tina? They'll be mortified if they can't swap anything,' pointed out Maunagh as we walked through Ashton Court in the mist.

'We can put in bags and shoes and stuff. Or they could get things for other people.' I was sure my idea would be good for all of us, and give us a bit of a lift to see us through the winter months.

We both stopped and watched as two deer leapt the fence in front of us.

'Once they've had a couple of drinks it'll be all right, I suppose. I've got a few things I was going to throw out anyway,' said Maunagh.

'Clothes swap party – bring a bottle and things to swap!' ran my email. Good old Maunagh had offered to hold a soirée at her house, and had turned out several bagfuls of clothing into the bargain. I had read about this kind of thing in the States: there they called it a 'naked lady party', which sounded somewhat more exciting, or a 'swishing party'. I had looked online at the clothes–swap organisation called Swap-O-Rama-Rama, which advised on customising old clothes too. A million tonnes of textiles go to landfill every year; only 25% are recycled. I liked the idea of passing on skills: older people showing the younger how to find their way around a sewing machine. There was also a website for swishing in the UK, www.swishing.org, which sadly had no details of upcoming events, but it did set out the swisher's rules: bring at least one 'good' item you'll be proud to pass on, and arrange the room with rails, ladders or ropes for the many coat-hangers you expect. Bring a camera to record the fun, and arrange the spoils creatively into potential outfits with accessories. They mentioned bringing along jewellery, too, but sadly we agreed this wasn't a possibility for us.

All our female friends came along, lugging bin bags of stuff they were glad to be rid of. It was actually a lot of fun, sitting on the floor in a state of semi-undress, sorting through our own private jumble sale, and running off to try things on from time to time. I had more than I thought, as usual, to give away, and we all went home feeling pleased with ourselves. The next morning, resplendent in my new attire, I dragged the few unclaimed clothes to our local charity shop.

The charity shops in Clifton had very few things I could afford on my pound a day. As I gratefully put my heavy bin bags down, I wondered if they would survive in the face of such stiff competition from the likes of Primark. They were offering new stuff at less than the second-hand prices in Oxfam!

Walking more easily now, I continued thoughtfully on my way to work. I had read that since 1995, according to the Office for National Statistics, women's clothing has fallen in price by 34%. Other things too had fallen ridiculously in price: PCs had fallen by an amazing 93%, and even something as mundane as a vacuum cleaner had cheapened by 45% in just over a decade. The big stores with their knockdown prices on everyday stuff have made it less and less worthwhile to fix broken items or buy second-hand.

What the hell, if something's looking a bit shabby, just get a new one! In Tesco's a new kettle was a fiver, and jeans could be had for £3 in Asda. No point in fixing a broken zip or cleaning up a grubby appliance; another one, made in dubious conditions far overseas, was waiting on the High Street to take its place.

I passed Boots. There was a big three-for-two promotion advertised in the window. But what if you didn't like the shampoo or whatever once you'd tried a bit? Still two and three-quarter bottles to go! Even worse with food; no wonder such a lot of what we buy is wasted. I was suddenly beginning to come over a bit Freegan.

Would I be any happier with an extra half-a-dozen handbags, £2 a time in Primark? Where the hell would I put them all anyway? And what would it say about me, if I were a person who threw money at cheaply churned-out crap like that, only to throw it away again for a newer version?

Something had changed on the High Street. People weren't shopping for necessities. They bundled by me with bagfuls of 'bargains' from stores with goods piled high and rapidly replenished. This was smash-and-grab, hit-and-run shopping. Do it loud and fast and often. Come away feeling you've made out like a bandit. That's the satisfaction which is craved, by rich and poor alike. Be proud that it's new, it cost less than a fiver, and if you change your mind about it you'll throw it in the bin on the way home!

I had been surprised to hear that Primark has been going since the early seventies. Discounting of goods by shops really took off back in 1964, when resale price maintenance was abolished. They were no longer held back by the law, and could compete more vigorously with one another. All it took then was for the British snobbery against cheapness, which was perceived as being déclassé, to evaporate along with the loose change at the checkout. People with time and money to spend, rather than those who were on the poverty line, were at the front of the queue.

Have we ever lived in 'Rip-off Britain'? I didn't think so. OK, food was dearer, relatively speaking, when I was a student, but then you could get a grant that didn't have to be paid back. And bedsits, albeit grotty, were about £8 a week…

Back in those days people attempted to get around high prices by smoking roll-ups, brewing their own beer, gardening and bringing back food and drink from shopping trips to France. The seeds were being sown then for British people to recognise their power as consumers: we were just beginning to learn to travel and shop around. We realised we didn't have to be meek and accept the going rate. And once the Internet got going, and we could search for the best price on an item without even going out of the front door, we had the retailers on the run.

While Easyjet led the boom in something-for-nothing travel, Primark did the same for clothing. And supermarket chains were cutting each other's throats for a penny here or there, meaning millions per day across their empire. The customers treat it like a war, too: we are proud of our victories over the system. On the radio the other day a pseudo–scientific term had made me smile: 'compulsive price disclosure'. My parents, I remembered, used to be very, very coy about the cost of things they had bought. And they would never in a million years discuss their income. My students had always been taught that money, especially savings and salaries, was a big taboo here. But was that still true? I felt it was beginning to change.

I tramped on up the hill, avoiding A-frame signs which littered the pavement in everybody's way, trying to lure us in to this or that shop.

Passing an estate agent, it struck me that the only thing that was really getting more expensive was housing. I had recently read an interview with David Mitchell, spokesman and technical director of the Home Builders Federation. He had been quoted as saying that property developers are now 'keeping new houses as small as possible to keep the price down'. Old terraces like mine were being chopped up into flats. And, of course, storage space was being reduced as a consequence. 'It is a worry,' Mitchell said. 'Eventually something's got to give between how much we own and how much space we live in.'

I knew of people who had bought garden sheds, which luckily don't need planning permission, to fill their outdoor space with more room for storage. And the enormous warehouse of storage units near where I lived was doing a roaring trade, renting spaces scarcely bigger than a phone box for the same amount as I paid for my room in a shared house.

An enormous lorry was blocking the road outside the Tesco Metro, while the staff unloaded another shipment of frozen food. I stepped into the road to avoid the mêlée on the pavement, and noticed that it was the same for the shops: their space was all given over to displaying their wares, so the lorries had to keep on coming, day and night, to replenish the shelves. More pollution. More traffic. More environmental damage. Just so we could buy stuff cheaply.

But not everything was cheap. I couldn't afford to live alone: the council tax would be too dear, even with a single person's discount. And I was out here putting in mile after mile on foot because the buses were so expensive in Bristol. The Office of National Statistics said that rail prices had risen on average by 36% since 1995, and petrol by 63%. It wasn't surprising I couldn't afford the council tax either: they said it had risen on average by 100%! So goods were getting cheaper but services (at least, those which can't be done for us by countries which pay their workers less) were getting more expensive. That's why so many of my friends were in such a financial pickle: university fees, pensions, mortgages, fuel bills. Were they buying endless 'bargains' to forget their bigger woes?

'In Slovakia, my parents used to save up for fear of costly times ahead. I prefer to spend now, because I may not be able to if hard times are on the way!' said Lilli.

'I think that's where a lot of my friends are coming from,' I agreed. We were in her office and this was my last-but-one session with her. Lilli had become a great confidante and I respected her judgement immensely. She had helped me enormously to improve myself and think about what I was doing with my life. I knew, once she was qualified, that she would be a red-hot life coach.

'Have you organised another date for a clothes party? That's one way you can all get the satisfaction of having new things without spending money,' she asked.

'The next thing we're going to do is a wish-list and a gift-list,' I said.

She laughed. 'What are those?'

'Well, we go around our houses and just write a list of all the stuff we've got that we wouldn't mind giving away. I've got loads of books – too many to carry – and two woks when I only need one, and a few pictures I'm tired of, which could be used for the frame. That kind of thing.'

'So that's a gift list. And do they come and pick it up?'

'If they can. Or I could go to them and get some of their bits and bobs at the same time,' I said.

'And the wish list?' Lilli looked intrigued.

'It could be anything! I'm after a new bike lock, for instance. And my toaster's broken. I'm using the grill, but I'll ask on the wish list if anyone could have a go at fixing a toaster.'

'Not only things to give away, then, but help with things,' said Lilli.

'Yes, for instance I've already agreed to proof-read a dissertation for somebody. I can do that pretty easily, and it costs loads to get someone professional to do it.'

'I was going to ask you a favour, actually, talking of writing,' said Lilli, 'if I could add a wish to the wish list! Do you think you could write a letter of recommendation for me? I could add it to my portfolio for prospective clients.'

'Course I will! I'll bring it next time,' I said, shrugging back into my coat.

As I walked home through the fog I thought about what to write in my last 'homework' for Lilli. I was so deep in thought that I almost walked into a fridge, abandoned on the pavement. A note was stuck to it: 'council collecting Tuesday.' It didn't look very old, but once they were broken they weren't worth fixing. And they were notoriously difficult to dispose of, thanks to the environmentally unfriendly gases within. It was a problem, I reflected, that we all wanted to be paid a lot for what we did, and it made it hard to get repairs done at a reasonable price. I'd enquired about my toaster in a Bedminster shop that did electrical repairs, just for academic purposes, and found that the repair would be 'about £17'. In nearby Tesco's, a Value Two Slice Toaster was £4.44. My curiosity was piqued, and I asked him for more quotes on fixing everyday items. Obligingly he rattled off some ballpark figures: a kettle: £15. A DVD player: about £60. A steam iron: £15. A vacuum cleaner: about £60. Sadly, he seemed to have plenty of time to chat, since there was nobody else in the shop and nothing waiting for his attention. I wondered how long he would be able to remain in business at that rate. On the High Street, I priced a new kettle: a fiver, also in Tesco. New DVD players were £25 in Woolworths, and irons £9 in Marks and Sparks. Vacuum cleaners were to be had for £30 in Woolies, and Currys had new stuff which would just make a joke out of hauling your old appliances in to a repair shop or paying a workman to come out and look at them.

What were we all going to do? There was only one thing for it, I decided as I opened the door into our chilly darkened house. We would have to learn to be better at sharing.

December

I boycott the Christmas post, develop an allergy to mince pies, and have a really hard time persuading people not to treat me in the festive season. I learn about 'Froogles' and how to share with others.

I was struggling with a pâté pot when I heard a noise at the front door. A bit of rustling, a bit of groaning. I dashed out and flung the door open to reveal the postman, bent double, trying to force a package through the inch-high space below it.

'Sorry, our letterbox is tiny, isn't it?' I said with a smile.

'Trouble is, there's no porch to leave it in. So I carries it all the way back if nobody answers,' he said.

'Lucky I was in then!' I said, wondering why he hadn't rung the doorbell. I sorted out my mail from the wad he handed me and went back excitedly to my room to unpack the booty. A trial-size bottle of mint shower gel, another of anti-dandruff shampoo, and a Charlie Chaplin DVD. All mercifully unbroken by the postman's endeavours. I'd been signing up for free samples and trial offers in earnest over the past couple of weeks, and had amassed quite an impressive haul. I was in the middle of making Christmas crackers out of toilet roll cores and recycled paper, and putting miniature toiletries inside. So many of the beauty counters in town had sachets of moisturiser or make-up to give out, now that the party season had arrived. I was assembling little 'weekend kits'

85

for my crackers, which I thought looked rather nice tied up with cellophane and ribbons cut from old clothes using pinking shears.

Last year's decorations had been dug out from under my bed, but they wouldn't go up until the last possible moment: too much to live with in one room for more than a few days. As for those glass pâté pots all the way from the Calais hypermarket, they were now filled with tinfoil, a decorated candle in each one. I had unearthed paint and glitter to turn my white candles into something festive.

I was beginning to succumb to the excitement of the season. It was great to have a chance to be creative on a pound a day, and to see if anybody noticed my lack of spending power.

Good thing green-ness is in fashion, I thought, buffing over the cover of a second-hand book with a cloth misted in furniture polish. There might be brownie points for saving the planet in imaginative ways rather than speculation over my stinginess!

There was quite a collection of goodies in my room these days: bric-a-brac such as a pair of brass candlesticks bought for 20p in a charity shop, now polished and shiny; second-hand cocktail glasses picked up for pennies, newly sparkling and filled with sweets with a clingfilm cover; giveaway books, mugs and CDs, and samples of everything from shoe polish to salad dressing. I would wrap them as prettily as possible. My irrepressible urge to hoard things had paid off: there was lots of last year's wrapping paper plus tissue and coloured plastic I'd collected over the last few months. I even had the cards I had received last year, thoughtlessly boxed up with the decorations. With my pinking shears and a hole punch I made a collection of gift tags out of the old cards.

Christmas cards themselves were a bit trickier. Not the making of them, which I loved, but the postage. Stamps were a great luxury on my budget; I wouldn't be able to use the help of the Royal Mail this time. But I still wanted to give a token card and keep in touch. I sat down and made a list of everyone I wanted to send a card to. A few were overseas, others scattered around the country, the majority in or near Bristol. Not many would be satisfied with an E-card, not even an especially personalised one using Photoshop. But those who wouldn't mind that, I put in one column. Those around Bristol, I could reach by bike and hand-deliver to. The next weekend I was hitching to my father's. I would take to him the presents and cards for all the family, because he would be meeting them at my brother's house party on Christmas Eve.

That just left half-a-dozen cards to post. Okay, one of the recipients would be visiting before the 25th. I crossed her off. And if I made an especially lightweight card for my American aunt and her family, I could ask my dad to post it in with his…

Only four stamps to buy, then. Not bad out of over fifty cards. And the leg-work of delivering them all would certainly keep me fit!

The house party at Dan and Sarah's would have tested my ability to keep my challenge a secret, especially with the drinks flowing. Luckily, I had already made plans: I had booked myself up to house- and pet-sit for two Bristol friends, with a round of other houses to go to over the holidays, feeding people's cats while they were away. My break from school was for over a fortnight, but it was sure to pass quickly. I was going to do my hedge-laying workshop with the BTCV, volunteer on the charity gift-wrapping stand in Debenhams, and help out at a street fair in Clifton.

Heather and I went to a carol service at her local place of worship. It was as good as karaoke, we agreed afterwards over a glass of (free) mulled wine. There was something very satisfying about singing, loud and lustily, those long-familiar songs. We became the local carol tarts, hopping from church to church, grabbing candles and jingling small change into the collection plate as we sang all the Victorian favourites, off-key but with great enthusiasm. We learned from leaflets and notice boards that many congregations enjoyed free choral, orchestral or organ concerts all year round, plus public speakers and debates: another list of events to add to my diary. Heather and I drank in the atmosphere, the art and architecture, and of course the complimentary beverages.

Then there were the mince pies. Not my favourite thing. But how hard to avoid! Queuing for my precious four second-class stamps behind people laden with packages costing a tenner apiece to post, I had mince pies pressed upon me by the Indian post office proprietor's daughter. Taking a short cut through Marks and Spencer's, they were pushed under my nose to sample. Boozy ones. Iced ones. Big fat cheap ones. Every breed of shop was reminding its customers what time of year it was, so they would lay aside their spending inhibitions and whip out the credit card. Oh, the power of the mince pie! I ate literally dozens. And at Gordano Services, starting out on the hitch-hike to visit my father in the Midlands, a car going in the opposite direction stopped and a young woman got out. Risking life and limb in the roundabout traffic, she ran over to me and handed me a red cardboard box. Of mince pies.

My dad, fortunately, is quite partial to them. He sat nibbling one with his cup of tea as we caught up.

'You won't meet Sarah's parents until the wedding then, probably,' he was saying.

'No, not unless they come down again in the spring. You'll have to tell me about them,' I said, rubbing my shoulder. The bags of presents had been heavy to hitch with.

'I'm driving to Cambridge on Christmas Eve morning. Hope it's not as foggy as last year,' he said through a mouthful of pastry.

'Well, I don't think there's much chance of snow! It's really warm outside still. Do you want to come out for a walk?'

'Yes, why not?' said Dad, finishing his tea. 'Where do you want to go?'

'Actually,' I said, producing half a dozen envelopes, 'I wanted to drop cards in to a few of my old school friends…'

Added to the weight of my luggage were the ingredients of a casserole. I threw everything into the pot, put it in the oven, and then we went out into the dark to deliver cards and admire people's fairy lights and decorations through their windows. I was struck by how little anything changed up here: it was stuck in a time-warp compared to Bristol, still celebrating the season in a modest way. I remembered our childhood celebrations at my father's house: our excitement was as high as the budget was low. We had real stockings – my mother's – with satsumas in the toes. School stationery was mixed in with other practical things like gloves and socks and soap-on-a-rope. The big presents were books or jigsaws. We didn't have lots of toys, but we didn't seem to miss them. I smiled to myself in the darkness. This year I was indulging in a rather retro festive season.

What present do you get for someone who's living on a pound a day? To those of my friends who asked, I suggested they pass on to me something they had already, rather than spending money. In this spirit I got thoughtful and imaginative gifts: a hair and makeup session from Maunagh, a book Janet and I had talked about after she read it, two cassettes of Neil's best party mix music and a selection of invitations to a 'storecupboard supper'. A couple of well-meaning people gave me book tokens and Boots vouchers. That was the same as giving money, I thought. Accordingly, I stashed them away for the distant future. The rest of the world, who didn't know my secret, disquieted me with invitations to the pub or to a restaurant to celebrate the holiday. Of course, I had to plead prior engagements, and invite them to one of my free events instead. It was fortunate that they never got together to work out that I hadn't been for a meal in a restaurant for over six months, or to the pub either, apart from a quick chat over a glass of soda water.

Booze was not, however, in short supply. All the people I cat-sat for, in spite of my protests that the perishable contents of their fridge were enough recompense, left me a bottle of wine. A whole caseful arrived from Dan and Sarah, and mulled wine seemed to end every event we attended. With mince pies, of course. So to use it all up, there was nothing for it but to have a house party. Pity I didn't have a house, though... Fortunately for all the people whose property I was minding, I had other friends generous enough to lend me theirs, and so in the run-up to Christmas we all got together.

'Are you getting used to it now?' asked Helen, poking the brazier in her garden with a stick.

'I find it harder and harder to imagine going back to how I was before,' I said, moving my chair back as the flames rose higher.

'Nothing you miss?' asked Nigel, coming over with another armful of wood.

'Coffee shops.' I passed the wine bottle over to him. 'But I'm ashamed now to think how much time and money I wasted in them. Every week!'

Shrieks of laughter sounded from the lounge. Through the patio doors we could see Bern doing a comedy striptease to the strains of Madonna. The dancing was in full swing; nobody was feeling the cold.

'All fast asleep!' called Tina, advancing unsteadily onto the patio. She had been checking on everybody's kids upstairs.

'It's great, this age. They still haven't got to the stage where they want big presents like their friends,' said

Helen. 'I don't know what we'll do when that happens.'

'We're just not thinking about it. Not having a telly's good — stops them getting brainwashed,' said Nigel, knocking back his wine. He nodded towards the lounge, where Bern and Neil were trying to outdo each other in a silly dancing contest. 'And the best things in life are free, you know. Anyone up for a dance?'

With fun times like this, the holiday passed rapidly. It had meant a few compromises and a bit more effort than previous years, plus unfailing support from my ever-generous friends. We had a fine collaborative Christmas dinner, a walk in Ashton Court, a karaoke house-party for New Year, a winter picnic in a city park. There were lots of links on the internet to places where the householders had put up astonishing displays of festive lights, but it seemed a bit extravagant to drive around looking at them, even if they were collecting for charity. And the streets I walked around had some pretty nice decorations, after all. I watched no TV at all, but read a few books. It didn't seem boring or austere, though I did notice people stopping themselves when they began enthusing about going to see *Swan Lake*, eating in a new bistro, or picking up a bargain outfit in the Boxing Day sales. Really, I didn't mind hearing about their spending sprees. It just seemed a million miles away from my life now.

It was New Year's Day, quite warm and still, but I shivered a little as I crossed the Suspension Bridge. I was walking back from Long Ashton, and feeling slightly the worse for wear: singing karaoke all night and not getting any sleep had taken its toll. Once the hosts' children woke up, it was the cue for the last guests to leave.

It would be much harder to live on a pound a day with kids, I mused. Apart from their many needs, there were also their multifarious wants, as Helen and Nigel had said. And I would be inflicting my radical principles on someone who depended on me for everything. Would the Social Services be called in? Chuckling to myself, I arrived on the Bristol side of the bridge.

On impulse, I climbed uphill to the Observatory. The view was terrific: on one side, the green open spaces of the Downs, on the other, Bristol in all her brash urban glory. And far below, the Avon Gorge. This was where nature met mankind, and they blended well, with Brunel's bridge symbolising our attempts to control our environment and exploit it for the public good. In his day, resources must have seemed bottomless, all there for the taking.

Back in October, flushed with triumph after my trip to France, I'd read a discarded copy of the *Independent*, which carried an article about 'Froogles' in Bournemouth. Less extreme than the Freegans of New York, these were people who used the internet to cut consumerism to the minimum. Their motivation was to save the planet for their children (who were less than grateful, apparently). The woman interviewed was making soap and exchanging goods and services for nothing, among her friends and family and online. She had an allotment and kept hens, bought her clothes in charity shops, shared, bartered, and lent out her car. All very worthy stuff. She did, however, allow herself to buy new underwear and toiletries, pharmaceuticals and 'health products', whatever that category included. And food, of course, albeit unprocessed and local wherever possible. I had noticed recently that many of my friends were now attempting to do the same to some extent. They'd watched me go from shopper to Scrooge in the space of six months. If for no other reason than that they were impressed by the money I'd saved, they wanted to give the lifestyle a try.

I was lucky: so far I'd stayed fit and healthy, aided no doubt by an un-fancy diet and a lot of walking and cycling. If I did get ill, or need a dentist, I was prepared to spend money to safeguard my 'health and safety', as the *Independent* called it. But so far, so good.

For me, 'International Buy Nothing Day' in November had meant little; I'd cycled into town to sign a pledge at a stall run by a group of dreadlocked environmentalists. They were offering free snacks and books; I donated a few of my own and turned for home. Most of my days were Buy Nothing Days, after all! Nor did I tell them about the six months I'd just spent or the months awaiting me; I'd learned by now that awe and disbelief would follow. I just wanted to get on with it, to make it a lifestyle.

'The Compact' in San Francisco had done just that. A group of fifty professionals vowed to fly in the face of American consumer culture, in the pioneering spirit of the Mayflower Compact. They agreed to reduce waste, resist corporatism and support local enterprise. They had made it through 2006, and as far as I knew, they weren't stopping there.

Waste, my parents had dinned into me, was a Bad Thing, and it was even more so now on my budget. At this time of year everybody seemed to be buying up large, just in case of visitors, or so as not to appear stingy. And as the fridges told me in the houses where I was minding pets, a lot of food was heading straight for the bin. The *Daily Telegraph* reported that 6.7 million tonnes of food was thrown out by domestic consumers every year: a third of what is bought. And at least half of what was disposed of was still edible.

'Wrap', the waste reduction agency supported by the Women's Institute, claims that food wastage is a bigger problem than packaging disposal. This is because food decomposition releases the most potent of greenhouse gases, methane. The food supply chain is responsible for a fifth of UK carbon emissions, so reducing the amount of discarded food has got to be done. Besides, it costs every household £250 to £400 a year. And carbon is used to produce that food in the first place.

The W.I. seems like a good organisation to get us to jolly well pull our socks up. They bring to mind wartime connotations of austerity and cunning use of leftovers. Stale bread? Bread and butter pudding. Or breadcrumbs for something else. Old mash and veg. from that huge Christmas feast? Bubble and squeak, of course! The meat goes into a shepherd's pie, the fruit into a chutney, anything half decent into the freezer.

Now that food shortages are a distant memory in Britain, we tend to over-cater all the time, not just in the festive season. Perhaps if we understood more about where food comes from and what it costs to produce environmentally as well as financially, we'd value it more and make sure that we bought only what we needed, eating it all up before shopping for more. I was doing very well out of other people's wasteful habits, but I needed a bit of help!

I had been intrigued to read that the Froogles were helping each other via the internet. They 'freecycled' unwanted possessions without resorting to cash, area by area, requesting or offering as space or necessity dictated. Then there was 'Agenda 21' with articles advising local groups on composting, car-shares and solar energy. Or 'downsizer.com' inviting people to reduce what they had and share what was left. Just my cup of tea; I had to get around to taking a look at them.

I gazed across the sprawl of Bristol. All around, thousands of people would soon be waking up to their hangovers and wondering how to pay the next credit card bill after the excesses of the season. I wasn't going back to all that. For the New Year, I made two resolutions: not to take any flights, even after my pound-a-day challenge was finished, and to sign up to Freecycle.

January

I go public on living on a pound a day, receive some welcome advice and unwelcome attention, and get my 30 seconds of fame without (quite) dying of boredom. More free events are graced with my presence.

I waited for my boss to pull himself together. He produced an enormous blue handkerchief from the pocket of his chinos, and wiped his eyes. His face was flushed and his breathing laboured.

'But – you look so *healthy!*' he wheezed. 'How've you got away without telling anyone?'

I had finally admitted, in my New Year's appraisal at work, what I'd been up to this past six months. He was finding it vastly amusing.

'I've told my friends but not my family. I've got to save for my brother's wedding. That's why I'm doing it.'

'Really! Well, I for one didn't have a clue,' he chuckled. 'Though' – a thought struck him – 'you've seemed very enthusiastic about the social programme lately. Must be all the free drinks!'

While he enjoyed his own joke to the full, I reflected on what an admission like this would mean to my appraisal. There was clearly nothing he could offer in terms of financial incentive to improve my performance. I was practically saying that I turned up every day just because I *liked* it – wasn't I?

I said this out loud. He was pleased.

'There aren't many people who genuinely enjoy what they do, but you've proved it! I'm impressed.'

'I know I could've taken a year's sabbatical or something, but I really do appreciate my work. And my colleagues. And besides, it wouldn't be real life, giving up work to see if I can do this.'

'Are you going to tell people now?'

'Yes, I wanted to go a few months to see if anyone at work guessed, but now I've told you, I'll tell everybody.'

'Thank goodness for that! I don't think I could avoid mentioning it!'

My appraisal, then, went pretty well. The boss ended by exercising his curiosity about how my new lifestyle was conducted: what was permitted and forbidden and so on. It was a relief not to have to keep it quiet any longer; my workmates were friends too, after so many years in the school together. But I did wonder if they would think back to all those dinner invitations I'd turned down, or the collection envelopes I'd sheepishly jangled coins into. By the time I left the office, they'd all gone home, but when I arrived the next day it was clear that word had spread.

'She's a dark horse, this one!' said Clara in her broad Scottish brogue.

'Have you really not cheated? Even at Christmas, or when you've got pissed and passed a kebab van?' This was from Simon.

'She could have blagged one for free! I've done that, chatted the bloke up. He gave me a kebab to get rid of me!' said Elena.

Nobody looked surprised to hear this, so she went on. 'We've hitched back to Redland and all sorts!'

'I've been hitch-hiking around,' I admitted.

'You haven't!' said Sue, appalled. 'It's so dangerous!'

'That's how I got to France last year. It was fine.'

'You mean – to go on holiday – you hitched? And still just spent a quid a day?' asked Joe.

'That's right. It's still possible.'

And so the astonishment carried us through coffee time and lunchtime, and on and on after school was over. I was gratified that they hadn't guessed my secret, but a little taken aback by the extremity of their reaction.

'So why are you going public now?' asked Elena. 'Someone might jump in and steal your idea before you've finished the year!'

'They're welcome to – the more the merrier! I didn't want to keep it a secret really; it was just to test how obvious it was that I was living on so little.'

'Well, not at all, clearly!' said Clara. 'But I don't think I'd be able to do what you're doing. I'm too impulsive.'

I laughed. 'It was being too impulsive that got me into this in the first place!'

'Are you repenting at leisure now?' asked Sue.

'I think it's one of the best things I've ever done. It's taught me a lot about myself. That and the life-coaching.'

'Life-coaching? How did you afford that?'

And so the questions went on. There was a great deal of brainstorming of ways to get along without spending money. Everybody had an idea to help: an organic butcher who gave chicken carcasses away for a donation in the

99

charity box, a market research company that gave tea and biscuits while interviewing respondents. Or blood donation for the same reward. Hmm. Perhaps that was a freebie too far.

They had a couple of great suggestions, though: I had an old mobile phone which no longer worked. Somebody told me about Envirofone, where you can look up the cash value of the handset online (it wasn't much, but better than nothing), then send off for a Freepost envelope and labels. A while later you get a cheque, and the phone is recycled, not wasted. Following their advice, I put the money into my emergency fund and forgot about it.

Of course, electrical equipment, batteries too, can be recycled if they carry the crossed-out wheelie bin logo. And soft furnishings can be collected by charities such as The Sofa Project, as long as they have a fire safety label.

My colleagues advised me to improve on draught-proofing in our un-insulated Victorian house to save on fuel bills. I hung a heavy curtain over the door, and made an old-fashioned draught excluder sausage from the leg of a pair of tights stuffed with old clothes. It blocked the gap under the door very well. Because I was living on a pound a day, I didn't use any heating in my room the whole winter. Almost half the UK's CO^2 emissions come from the energy we use at home or while travelling, so I tried to do my bit not to add to the problem of climate change. It helped my landlady to save money too. Although I was out a lot, I tried to be conscientious about switching things off. I didn't want to create any more waste than I had to while saving up for June.

'Why are we doing this?' asked Maunagh, shivering. We were standing in a queue outside a coach. Inside the firmly closed doors, the driver read a newspaper and ignored his wretchedly cold passengers with enviable disdain. We were outside the Students' Union, and the queue to get on consisted largely of students drawn by the posters advertising an entirely free event: a bus to take us there, a buffet with drinks when we arrived, then a rip-roaring evening of entertainment, being recorded for TV while hob-nobbing with the stars. How could someone living on a pound a day ignore it?

The BBC has a website for free tickets to shows, and Channel 4 too, plus there are opportunities for those who would like to be a contestant on such classics as The Weakest Link. Embarrass yourself in front of strangers! Enjoy being criticized while millions watch and chuckle! I, too, began to wonder belatedly what on earth I thought I was doing.

At last the driver deigned to let us in. He was clearly expecting nothing in the way of tips for this job. We proceeded to steam up the windows with our coats damp from the drizzle, while an extremely young researcher from the TV company took the microphone and attempted to fill us with enthusiasm. We were cold and hungry, but did our best to seethe with anticipation.

It was just a short journey to the Endemol studios, where we joined another queue of people who had made their own way there.

'I feel a bit like I'm in Communist Russia,' I muttered to Maunagh. 'See a queue and join it, just in case there's anything worth having at the end!'

'There'd better be – I'm starving!' she replied.

Slowly, we edged inside, through a check-in process and a cloakroom system, to a very overheated room with a large buffet, and wine to be administered in help-yourself fashion into plastic cups. We fell on this like a plague of locusts, making an impression to be proud of on the piles of sandwiches and hot snacks. After all that, we were thirsty, so we elbowed the students and the polite older people out of the way and got on with the wine, which was rough but refreshingly cold. Because of all this, when a little silver-haired fellow materialised and stood at the doors surveying the scene, it took us a few moments to register that it was Noel Edmonds.

Deal or No Deal is considered by many to be an absolutely riveting show; the ratings confirm it. Back then, it was in its early days, but even coming to it fresh, having never seen the game on the telly, Maunagh and I agreed that it was one of the most boring experiences we had ever lived through. Never mind that there was a break after the recording of the first show, during which we could numb ourselves with more wine and food. We still had to go back and sit through more of the same excruciating nonsense all over again! In the second show, we were asked to come up and open the boxes for the viewers' competition, but apart from enjoying a bit of a rest from the unforgiving studio chairs, we remained unmoved. I did dare to suggest to the juvenile researcher that the whole thing could be videoed and watched on fast-forward without losing any of the content or atmosphere, but she didn't seem to get my point. And the contestants, and most of the guests apart from ourselves, were having a whale of a time. Our favourite part, in fact, was before the show began, when the audience was asked to act out some emotions for the cameras. 'Look delighted!' yelled the researcher, and we all turned and beamed to one another. 'Now – disappointed!' And we obligingly groaned and rolled our eyes. It seems that these shots of audience reaction are inserted later, to make it appear that we were all deeply engaged in what was happening, and having an absolute humdinger of an evening. I can't say for sure – I was so traumatised by the boredom, I could never bring myself to watch the programme at home.

So after that, what on earth possessed me to go back and participate in other shows? Well, partly it was pure greed. The catering contractors for Endemol entertainment do a terrific job. The Green Room at Channel Four was all right, but very modest in comparison, when I went on a crossword-solving show for them. That was a last-minute favour to a friend who worked there; two of the contestants had let them down, and he knew I liked crosswords, so could I possibly…?

It was quite fun really. The other stand-in turned out to be one of the Channel 4 canteen chefs, with a shirt from Wardrobe hastily ironed and thrown on, and his chequered trousers hidden behind the contestants' podium. The top prize was £3,000, which would have caused me a bit of a moral dilemma, but clearly there was no chance I was going to win. The lovely lady in a wheelchair who scooped the money watched the show every day, did crosswords day and night, and had travelled from somewhere north of

Birmingham and spent the night in a hotel with her carer. We all went away happy that day, although for weeks afterwards people kept coming up to me, asking, 'Didn't I see you on TV the other day?'

Then there was the sad fact that Maunagh has got a soft spot for Les Dennis. Because we'd been on Deal or No Deal, the studios emailed me about his new show, In the Grid. I mentioned this to her, expecting her to shriek in horror at the thought of going back there, but this time she insisted on our going through it all again. He seemed a very nice man, actually. Neither of us understood the game any better at the end of it than we had at the beginning, but we had a bellyful of wine, got moved to the front row, and Maunagh got a few words with the man himself. Thus we passed our few minutes of fame. But would I go back again now? No deal!

The school social programme had some fun evenings for the students in which I took part: anything from a walk in the old city to a night in a club. But my personal favourite had to be the International Food Party. This was held in a church hall, and the students worked individually or with friends to create a dish from their country's cuisine. They carried foil-covered plates and Tupperware containers through the streets from their homestay accommodation, no doubt leaving the kitchens there in chaos, and shared the results of their labours with their schoolmates. The buffet that ensued was always a roaring success: lukewarm curry nudged lovingly prepared sushi; mountainous German desserts jostled with borscht and bread-and-butter pudding. The school provided beer and wine, with a mix of world music in the background. We all stumbled home feeling slightly queasy but full of international good feeling.

It was good to keep active during the long dark evenings. I didn't spend a lot of time around the house, or around my friends' houses either. Instead, I met them in our favourite bookshops. Borders was the best since it stayed open until 10pm and provided comfy chairs for the book-reading or chatting clientele. If we got hungry, we'd pop over to Fresh and Wild and browse their ever-generous samples, get a cup of hot water from Starbucks or drink nice samples of herbal tea and hot cordial in Culpeper. This enchanted triangle of shops was friendly not only to students from the adjoining campus, but to frugal people like ourselves. We had all shopped from them in the past, and knew we would again, so we didn't feel like freeloaders. Nor were we ever treated that way: the staff were unfailingly pleasant as we browsed and loafed and mooched for many a happy evening. There was a whole tribe like me: faces I grew to recognise, leafing through the magazine shelves without making a purchase, browsing in Waterstone's, sheltering from the rain in Blackwells on a sofa or keeping in touch on the library computers. I was only living for a year like this – it had been a conscious choice and I would doubtless return to my (sensible) buying habits – but for many I could see it had long been the way they got by.

Venue magazine was invaluable in keeping me in touch with events in Bristol: lots of them were free, if you just sought them out. (Naturally, I didn't buy the magazine, but made surreptitious notes in bookshops or from other people's copies.) Obscure galleries had opening nights: I traversed the Gloucester Road, Stoke's Croft and St. Paul's, far from my own patch, to go to open studios and art events I'd never have come across by chance. Every one was a surprise, and I often met fascinating people there. The artists were always delighted to see people swelling the turnout and adding to the colour of the proceedings. Quite often, on these long walks across the city, I'd come across coins which had been dented and battered all day by car wheels skimming them to and fro on the tarmac: roadkill money for my growing collection. Even if it was just a penny, I'd pick it up, but I was still finding larger denominations of coins, and notes, dropped from a careless hand onto the darkened streets. I remembered that, as a child, I'd often surprise my parents by spotting coins as we walked. They thought I was sharp-eyed, but perhaps it's just a matter of being closer to the ground. Or having less to concern yourself with above it.

Children's events were often worthwhile too: the City Museum had dance or music performances which weren't just nice for kids. The galleries too often had special tours or talks: I wrote them all in my diary and did my best to fit them in. If anyone was handing out leaflets, I'd cross the street to see what it was about. If there were posters up in the library or community centre, I'd go through them carefully, sifting through for entertainment or opportunity. Music students put on lots of performances for free; we were there. A new shop having a gala opening? I'd be straight in for a glass of bubbly and some live music. Bristol was an absolute treasure trove if you just knew where to dig.

I used to avoid market researchers, assuming that they would waste my time, hanging about on the street with a clipboard. My colleague Penny was right, though – times had changed, and now they offered incentives. I was led into a church hall and positioned in front of a laptop to watch an advertisement and answer questions about it on the computer. Much more pleasant than huddling in a doorway outside. And there were rewards! The least was a cup of coffee, but at other times they handed out vouchers or samples of the product we were testing. The best one of all was when I was offered a couple of litres of a new laundry detergent. I had to record its use over a fortnight then give my feedback to a representative who phoned after the trial period. It made a change from eking out a Smart Price Washing Powder from the 'reduced to clear' rack. It was only 25p because the box had been punctured, and it did the job. But the luxuriously fragranced 'mystery brand' I was testing, I had to admit, was deeply seductive after months of laundered clothes that simply smelled, well, not dirty.

Watching advertisements for market research was a bit surreal when I knew I had absolutely no chance of buying whatever the product was. It changed my attitude completely. On the one hand, I could appreciate the ads as works of art, tended with loving care by a dedicated team trying oh, so hard to please a chance observer. I was one of the last in a long and expensive process, offering up my reaction to someone's painstakingly developed idea.

On the other hand, it was easier, from my viewpoint, to see straight through the wooing and flattery designed to make me feel bereft without their product. They tried to persuade me it was made for someone like me. I *needed* it to show the world what I really was! Give it to me now! On this level, I permitted myself a cynical smile. People who live on a pound a day are above that kind of manipulation. We manipulate you right back, thumbing our noses at your marketing. Better give me the samples, then, because I'm never going to buy what you're advertising, just because you tell me to!

It was satisfying to identify, then separate, my wants and my needs, realising how little I really did need made me feel successful, wealthy and empowered − all those things the advertisements try to persuade you into thinking you'd get from them.

February

An amusing brush with death, a search for a working holiday without a price tag, a Wicked Thing I did with someone else's lost property, and breaking the pound-a-day rule for the first time.

The white cardboard coffin dominated the lounge. A group of women sat around it making small talk, passing around the nibbles. One of Phoebe's neighbours made to put a dish of olives down on the coffin lid, then stopped herself with a nervous giggle. Our eyes strayed back to its ominous, silent presence, again and again.

At last, two women came in. They were sombrely dressed and carried notebooks and a cassette recorder. We quietened expectantly as they moved to the head of the coffin and sat down.

'Welcome to Lifting the Lid!' one announced. 'Thank you all for coming, and agreeing to let us collect your thoughts and ideas about death this evening. As you know, we're preparing material for our stage performance next month, and we hope you'll all come along to see it as our guests.'

Her companion, who was heavily pregnant, pressed 'play' on the tape machine, and funereal music issued out. 'Please, don't be shy. And don't be ashamed to cry!' she said.

Maunagh and I began to get the giggles. I didn't dare to look at her, but could feel the sofa shuddering as she suppressed her amusement.

'First of all, perhaps we can go around and introduce ourselves, and say what brought us here,' the pregnant woman said.

What was I going to say? That I never turned down a free drink? That I fancied a night out at the theatre? I certainly didn't have any special story to tell about death or funerals.

It was a bit like Alcoholics Anonymous. The first guest stood up. 'Hi, I'm Jane, and I'm a neighbour of Phoebe's. She invited me here to her house because she knows I recently lost my father.'

'I'm Amanda. I work in a care home, so we deal with death and dying every day. I thought I could share my thoughts on working with people who are near the end of their lives.'

It was my turn. 'I'm Kath. I haven't lost anyone recently, but I was interested to find out what would happen at an evening like this. And I'm intrigued by the idea of a performance based on what we have to say.'

'Welcome, Kath,' intoned the pregnant one over the music. 'I hope we all come away with something to think about this evening.'

They introduced themselves and explained their mission: to de-mystify death, which they saw as a taboo subject in our society, and to 'lift the lid' on the emotions we Westerners tend to suppress in public when faced with a funeral. It was in fact a very enjoyable evening, although there were no emotional outbursts of any feelings except mirth from Maunagh and myself. The most intriguing part of the proceedings was when the coffin was opened to reveal a variety of personal objects: shoes, buttons, cigarettes, half-empty bottles of booze. Our task was to pick an object and explain why it reminded us of someone we knew who had passed away. And after that we had carrot cake.

The performance, when it was finally shown, contained quite a medley of our input: mime, quotes of our comments on dying, singing and dance. The audience was gratifyingly large and appreciative and we who had joined in with 'Lifting the Lid' felt unduly pleased with ourselves. Especially when we had an after-performance party to go to with, yes, more cake.

'If only death was always so much fun!' enthused Amanda the nurse, who had had a couple of glasses of wine. But actually, we were inclined to agree.

Just recently, I'd noticed people stopping themselves in conversation around me again. It wasn't because they were shy about mentioning their bargains in the sales any more; the whole world was skint, it seemed. Fine with me: I felt at home with all the window-shoppers, magazine-browsers and country walkers. My colleagues were having leftovers for lunch every day now too. There were far fewer newspapers and takeaway cups of coffee being carried in to the staffroom nowadays. Everyone was saving up, and not just to counterbalance the excesses of Christmas. It was the dark, dull time of year when thoughts turn to booking a holiday, and that was what my acquaintances avoided talking about in my presence. I couldn't possibly be planning anything on my budget, could I?

It wasn't very long since I'd come back from France, but having spent much of the Christmas break in Bristol, I too felt like getting away for a change of scenery. But I had to go somewhere that was absolutely free.

I started my search by Googling 'volunteer holidays' down at the library. Overseas placements meant an arduous hitching trip, with an unpredictable arrival time. The Easter before, I'd been on a marvellous holiday with a company called Englishtown. English speakers were invited to stay in hotel accommodation in out-of-the-way corners of Spain or Italy. There was a free coach from the nearest airport; volunteers just had to arrive there at the appointed pick-up time. Once in the little resort, local students of English, mainly business people, were immersed in the language all day every day, thanks to their foreign helpers. We 'Anglos' were from all walks of life and many Anglophone countries. We were paired off for one-to-one chats, put into discussion or activity groups and taken on excursions. It was both well organised and relaxing. We ate delicious food and drank unlimited wine with it. And for the people like myself, it was all completely free of charge. All that was required was that you got yourself to the airport meeting place. I'd done a week's stint in both Italy and Spain, and had a fantastic time, meeting many new friends and doing a lot of partying in the process. But making the rendezvous would be a near-impossible feat while living on a pound a day. Regretfully, I filed away Englishtown's email inviting me back to a host of exciting destinations. I would find something nearer to home, and reduce the travel stress.

I was startled to find how many organisations expected people to pay for the privilege of volunteering. Okay, there were admin. costs or contributions to the food bill, reasonably enough, but paying a couple of hundred pounds to work for free for a week was taking the mickey a bit, I thought.

Working on the land appealed to me. I would have a complete change from my work and enjoy fresh air and exercise in a new area. The WOOFer scheme (Workers on Organic Farms) sounded great, with free bed and board and enough time to explore the area. It was started in 1971 by a London secretary who advertised in *Time Out* magazine for people to help clear brambles with her on an organic farm. WOOFing is now a massive worldwide project. But you needed to pay a £15 membership fee. Furthermore, a lot of places wanted a longer time commitment than I was able to give. There were Danish schemes for volunteer fruit harvesters or Christmas tree farmers with free camping and food provided, and in the UK there were details of community orchards where you could volunteer to help with haymaking and pruning trees, among other things. But these activities were not until the autumn, and I wanted a break now!

Then, just as I was beginning to feel downhearted, I found an activity centre thirty-odd miles away in Somerset. They took school groups for days or weeks at a time, and also maintained extensive grounds with an organic kitchen garden. They were prepared to take a volunteer to help on the grounds for a week. Plus, they would provide a room in the staff accommodation block and three square meals a day. Perfect! I filled in the booking form for Easter and waited eagerly for their reply. Now I could join in the anticipation in the staffroom. And there was no need to save up to buy sunscreen or swimwear: I'd just need my oldest clothes and some hitch-hiking signs.

Meanwhile, I took myself out and about. There were city walks for free starting in the centre of Bristol, led by very knowledgeable volunteers. I looked up free bird reserves, county by county, and just once went over to Bath with a friend to walk dogs from the RSPCA shelter, over the downs. We nearly got our arms pulled off, with two furry friends each, but came back rosy-cheeked and muddy, with the warm glow from having made a little bit of happiness happen.

The weather was awful. There seemed to be a full two weeks where I got rained on every single day. Somehow, that's all right when you're out for a walk in the country; just part of the experience. Different, though, when you're forced to teach a class with your feet squelching and trousers clinging uncomfortably to you, your hair still damp in spite of a session upside-down under the hand dryer in the toilets. I came back from the Avon Gorge to Pill bike track looking like I'd got in the way of a muck-spreader one Saturday afternoon. There was a broad slick of mud, which had sprayed from my back wheel, all the way from my bum to the back of my neck. The colour of my trainers was indistinguishable, and it took a rinsing session of bike and rider in the backyard water butt, before anything was fit to bring inside. Nevertheless, it was a most invigorating experience, going down to the stormy waterfront at Pill. I was buffeted by the wind as I gazed out at the gulls riding the wind. Beneath a cosmetic layer of mud-freckles my cheeks were fresh and rosy. I never regretted going out on a day-trip like that.

Once outfitted in my wellies, with raincoat hood drawn tight, I was happy to walk all day. I'd got a book of walks around Bristol from the library, and had discovered some delightful viewpoints and hidden curiosities by following the many miles of footpath recommended by the author. It was my aim to do every walk in the book over the next few weeks. They varied from two to fifteen miles, so the whole book would cover a couple of hundred miles' worth of my favourite city. A bit of rain was certainly not going to put me off.

It was a different matter going to and from work, though. I took to carrying a change of clothes in a plastic bag, then making myself more respectable in the Ladies' when I arrived. But even then, getting drenched again on the way home did start to become a trifle wearing.

One day, I was going straight from work to a lecture at the university. For once, I got out of the building without encountering any precipitation. But it was too good to be true: halfway there, the heavens opened yet again.

I really couldn't face sitting out the lecture soaked to the skin. There wasn't time to wait for the shower to pass by loitering in a shop or gallery. And of course, I couldn't just buy an umbrella or another change of clothes. But perhaps I could borrow something...

A wicked plot hatched itself in my mind. I walked into a large bookshop, one of several in the area which had seats for browsers and a coffee bar. I marched up to the young man behind a computer at the enquiries counter.

'Excuse me, has anyone handed in a black umbrella, please?' I asked.

'Just a second, I'll go and check,' he said. He disappeared into the back of the shop and came out smiling a couple of minutes later.

My surprise and delight was absolutely genuine. 'Oh, someone handed it in!' I exclaimed. 'Thank you so much!' And I took the umbrella gratefully before striding back out onto the rain-lashed street.

A Bad Thing to do? I don't doubt it. But I didn't steal the brolly; I merely borrowed it to save my skin. And after the lecture I popped into the bookshop once more. I propped the umbrella in a corner, browsed the shelves for a few minutes, then pottered out again empty-handed. It did cross my mind that if the enquiries assistant, or anyone else, had seen me leave it, there might have been a rather embarrassing scene. Well, one black brolly looks pretty much like another, I reasoned. I could have made a silly mistake the first time around; I just hope nobody got soaked because of me, and that the rightful owner has now reclaimed their property. I remembered seeing a tub of umbrellas outside buildings in Japan: they were there for the borrowing. I wish we could institute a similar system of trust here!

All this taking of spare clothes to change into was putting a strain on my wardrobe. I could hardly keep up with the drying-out of things, and my room was beginning to resemble a Chinese laundry. What I needed, I decided, was a few disposable bits of clothing, and a couple more pairs of shoes, just to see me through the monsoon. I was wearing my socks two pairs at a time now, because they'd worn thin over the winter. My black clothes had all gone grey from being washed and washed again, and my light-coloured garments had taken on a dull tinge too. Thanks to the clothes swap party, I had a few half-decent top layers, but beneath those, I was a bit threadbare. I resolved not to be involved in any road accidents, as my mother had always warned me that if I was, I'd better be wearing respectable underwear…

So where could I get a few more things to wear? Charity shops were too expensive, and although I wasn't above checking out recycling bins, recently their contents had been floating within an hour of being put out for collection. There was just one thing for it: I'd have to go to a good old-fashioned jumble sale.

So far, I had avoided cheating at all on my pound-a-day rule. I'd never spent money in advance from the next days' budget, and had avoided such disasters as library fines or losing my purse. It had been extremely hard to save up enough to put credit on my mobile phone, and in consequence I'd been very stingy with it. I sent emails instead, from work or public computer, or hand-delivered notes and cards to my local friends. This required a degree of planning for social engagements. I didn't mind going back to pre-mobile conventions, but felt a bit guilty at being the callee rather than the caller, trying not to use the mobile if it could be avoided. Nobody seemed to mind except me, though.

I'd been lucky while pet-sitting: two of the households had deals on their landlines for free calls in the evenings and at weekends. I felt I'd made up a bit for the rest of the year when I devoted a few hours to chatting to people at Christmas. My correspondents who had no computer access had been especially neglected, so it was nice to mollify them a bit.

It seemed a simpler life, with a lot more time spent out of doors, and worked just as well as vitamins and gyms to keep me healthy. I hadn't needed medicines either, although I was prepared to go outside of my challenge to buy them if absolutely necessary. The students at this time of the year spread cold germs among each other almost continuously, but I had managed to keep colds at bay. If necessary, I had Helen's patent remedies to help: half a teaspoon of honey and lemon juice in warm water for a sore throat, or onion juice and honey steeped together for four hours for a cough.

I kept clean with the most basic of toiletries: 21p toothpaste, soap which cost 19p for three bars, shampoo which was 29p for a litre. All these were in my local Asda. They were Most Environmental Retailer of the Year, I discovered to my surprise. Helen had another tip for me there: they took coupons for other stores, and they're not that bothered if you're not actually buying the item the coupon is for, as long as they do in fact sell it. I wasn't sure I'd have the bottle to test that one out in front of a long line of tut-tutting customers, but I was impressed by her nerve.

They were the cheapest in town without a doubt. There was toilet paper for 40p a pack, though I often found better quality stuff at reduced prices in the 'whoops!' section of the store, along with boxes of tampons or sanitary towels at less than half price. If I ran short of these, there were always

118

panty liners at 22p a box. These cheap things seemed to work just as well as the branded products: I didn't have to resort to boiling rags as had been suggested at the beginning of my year. People had come up with other money-saving ideas since then, too: taking the (free) contraceptive pill without breaks, to avoid periods altogether, or getting a Mooncup. This washable device was supposed to last forever. Unfortunately, they were too dear to buy in the first place on my budget. Perhaps I'd get one after the year was over, for the sake of greenness. It would have been much better to buy ethical products in every case: biodegradable cotton tampons, recycled loo roll, fair trade coffee. But my time on a pound a day had taught me the salutary lesson that beggars can't be choosers. You've got to be pretty well-off to buy environmentally friendly products, and although I tried to get by on as little of everything as possible, I had to eat, and I had to use a few toiletries to remain socially acceptable. Green considerations were harder to keep in the picture when they cost a lot.

One thing I couldn't avoid paying for was dental care. My dentist had written to say I was due a check-up, so I had that, and a polish from the hygienist. It was the most expensive thing I'd done since the previous June, and I wondered if it was really necessary to go beyond a pound a day for this. I'd heard of people going to the dental school as guinea-pigs for students. However, given the extreme difficulty in getting an NHS dentist in Bristol, I didn't want to run the risk of getting struck off the list while I still had one. I would be facing an uncertain future, I decided, in shaky unqualified hands, so I bit the bullet (metaphorically speaking) and paid up.

At any rate, I wasn't going to go into debt for the sake of a few extra clothes to see me through a rainy spell. That Saturday, I scanned the local paper's small ads, then went up to Clifton in keen anticipation. There were two jumble sales with free entry, one at ten in the morning and the other at noon. I carried an almost empty backpack, a flask and sandwiches for lunch, and the ubiquitous raincoat. I was set for a whole day out. There was quite a knot of people outside the first church hall, and as I approached, the doors were unbolted and we jostled in.

I was overwhelmed by the tons of clothing, mountains of books and toys, and a whole curiosity shop's worth of bric-a-brac. It was a hell of a lot cheaper than the charity shops, and it even managed to beat Primark, but to my disappointment there was still very little within my price range. Never mind, I thought, I'll do my errands, have my packed lunch inside the shopping centre out of the weather, then carry on to the other church hall in Redland. Who knows, they might be a whole lot more inexpensive.

But there, the story was just the same. I could have bought plenty of books for 10p, but I had other sources of reading material, in better condition, at the same price or free. The clothes were very nice, clean and well-presented on rails, but not especially cheap. As for the bric-a-brac, nobody's birthday was coming up, so there was no need to hunt for a bargain there.

Thoroughly disheartened now, I retraced my steps across Whiteladies Road and trudged soggily back towards Clifton Village. I came once more to the first church hall I'd checked out, and saw a heavily-laden woman struggling out with her carrier bags. So it was still open, I thought. On impulse, I popped my head around the door, curious to see by how much those mountains of clothes had reduced. They were greatly diminished, but there was still a lot to do for the ladies who were beginning to pack garments away into bin liners.

'Come on in, we're not closed yet!' called one of the women as she struggled to force a coat into a black bag. 'Everything you see is 10p now!'

I could hardly believe my luck. Within minutes I was in possession of a pair of boots, a long hooded mackintosh, a velvet jacket for work and a couple of respectable tops. As an afterthought, I added a pair of lightweight trousers. They'd dry quickly and be easy to carry as spares.

Jubilant now, I splashed home to try things on and run a load through the washing machine. I'd learned a useful lesson: nobody wants to dispose of unsold goods in a charity sale any more than in a supermarket. If I ever went to a jumble sale again, it would be just before they closed.

As suddenly as they started, the rainy days were over. The winter had seemed shorter than usual, perhaps due to my being out and about a lot or to the necessity of planning my time in order to achieve maximum value from minimum spending power. This end of the winter was a good time for wellbeing taster sessions: I had half an hour of reflexology, an Indian head massage, a morning having a go at the Alexander technique. Janet and I went to a 'hypnotherapy evening' at a local alternative practice. The four therapists gave a presentation, then tried to drum up custom over a buffet. The sessions were very pricey, but we were interested in the thinking behind them: helping people to relax, to sleep better, to overcome stress. If there were any taster sessions for that, I was up for it.

At a local department store, I had a free manicure, and in another, a skincare assessment and make-up session. I got my hair cut and highlighted for free and attended a hair-and-fashion show sponsored by a local hair salon chain. Ann and I enjoyed the champagne and chocolates, and each of us came away with a goody bag of hair products. We had saunas, swims and sessions at the gym. I played my complimentary relaxation CD at night, and slept like a baby. Did I need help with my frame of mind? Well, when I saw a card in a shop window from a hypnotherapy student who was looking for clients for a free course of sessions, I decided to find out.

March

Relaxation without the stress of a bill to pay at the end, and learning the arts of skill-swap, signing up for freebies and doing exchanges via the amazing world of Freecycle.

I lay on the futon, trying to concentrate on the soothing background noises from a cassette player. They were country sounds: twittering birds, babbling brooks, lowing cattle. They almost – but not quite – drowned out the traffic outside, and the insistent mewing of a locked-out cat at the door.

'Now, I want you to take some deep, slow breaths. Feel the air filling your lungs, then slowly, gradually, let it all out. That's it. And again…'

Sara's voice was so calm and soothing, I began to drift away. I was taken on a walk, guided by her voice. It was a beautiful day. I crossed a meadow, followed a stream, and walked onto a deserted beach. Here, I lay in the sun while she told me a story about two trees. One swayed with the wind, enjoying the sensation of movement, while the other resisted with all its might. Finally, the stubborn tree learned to let go and allowed itself to move, along with the weather. Only then could it join the dance with the other trees, letting their branches be bent and shifted by superior forces. And accepting that so many things are beyond your control is the first step to inner contentment.

I listened to her soft voice for what seemed like few minutes. Then slowly, gently, Sara's voice brought me back to reality. I stretched and opened my eyes. To my surprise, the wall clock told me I'd been lying on that futon for over half an hour! Where on earth had the time gone?

There was no doubt that I was feeling relaxed, however. Hypnotherapy was all right by me if it made me feel this good. I floated away down the street in a haze of *joie de vivre*. I remembered all of the session, but for the life of me couldn't recall just which bit of it had been so invigorating. The chill, gloomy day seemed to have got a few degrees warmer. Next time, though, I'd listen out for clues as to how Sara had improved on my day so spectacularly. But the next time it was just the same. Perhaps it was simply the soothing quality of her intonation, or just the pleasantness of lying down in a warm, dark, safe place at the end of my working day. Whatever it was, I was hooked.

It was teeming with rain again when I dashed into the library, casting off damp layers as I headed for my booked computer. Today I'd taken a two-hour session. Before I began, I went over the noticeboards. There were 'meet up' groups advertising social evenings in other languages, in case I wanted to practise my Spanish or French. They organised films and talks too. I really had to get around to checking them out one day.

Skill swapping was posted up there too: in my neighbourhood you just joined a group for free, then either swapped skills directly through the website (like dog walking for house cleaning) or advertised a service and saved up points to 'pay' other skill-swappers with. My group's points are called 'Biscuits'. I'd signed up, of course, offering as many things as possible, including driving people in their own car to the airport and waiting for them on their return, proof-reading or babysitting. As yet, I hadn't had any requests for my services and the people I'd asked for help hadn't been available, but I was sure that sooner or later a skill swap would work out.

At the computer keyboard, I checked messages and sorted out my social life, then looked for free events in Bristol. There was quite a lot going on: the launch of a new photographic exhibition, an inaugural lecture, a lunchtime talk by a BBC wildlife presenter, and cheese and wine tasting at a newly opened bar in town. What was more, in a village within cycling distance, there was an art trail, kicking off with a buffet and drinks in the community centre, then touring the different venues in a free minibus shuttle. All these events duly went into my diary. I was getting good at finding them nowadays.

Now for the freebies. I opened the websites of all the big companies and often found links to sign up for free samples. Lots of my toiletries and sanitary products came to my door via this method, besides the little gifts I still collected for friends and family. Sites like Greasy Palm gave subscribers hints on where to look for free samples and special offers. It was also worth keeping an eye out to see which new products were being advertised on TV or billboards, then Googling them to get a free trial pack. But today all I found was teabags. Better than nothing, I thought, signing up and clicking on 'submit'.

There was still the best part of an hour left on my computer. Idly, I Googled 'Bristol recycled,' just to see what came up. And there it was: Bristol Freecycle, the group I'd made a New Year's resolution to join. Better late than never, I decided. I'd taken a while to get around to it because you needed to open a Yahoo account, then join the local Freecycle group through that. But after half an hour's palaver passwording and form-filling, my application was in. And a mere few days later, the postings started arriving in my inbox.

Why hadn't I done this before? There was just about everything there, being offered and requested: furniture, electronic items, vehicles, books, clothes, toys, food and drink, all higgledy-piggledy like a free virtual jumble sale. Anything that was not living and breathing, in fact, could go on the site. As long as it was destined for the landfill, working or not, complete or incomplete, it was Freecycleable. I was excited. The pickup area was mentioned in every case, and some of the things offered were far away, it was true, but they were always totally free to the collector. And how much better for everyone to have an eager new home for your junk, collected from the front doorstep. No more tiresome trips to the council dump! And judging by the 'received with thanks' messages, almost everything was grist to the mill. 'Received: quarter tin of magnolia paint.' 'Gone to a good home: dog bedding and old towels.' 'Taken: box of 2003 vintage women's interest magazines.'

Almost salivating in anticipation, I chose three of the most recent postings and typed a reply. Had they still got their size five trainers/assorted stationery items/selection of opened bottles of shampoo? I soon learned that you had to be quick to stand a chance of being chosen as the lucky recipient. In all three cases, the reply was, 'Sorry, gone.' But

I wasn't put off. By dint of judicious timing and a fair bit of legwork, I was soon the proud possessor of two kilos of green lentils, some slightly torn waterproof over-trousers, and the entire contents of an old lady's larder. She had been moved into a care home and her daughter was clearing her old flat out. Since the condition was that everything had to go, I made two heavy trips on my bike. Some of the food was years out of date. Stuff like tinned soup, I ate anyway. Other things, like suet and weevil-filled flour, I made into fat-balls to feed the birds in the back yard. Nothing went to waste, and I made cakes and biscuits with some of the in-date bakery products. I took them in to work, and my colleagues were pleasantly surprised; my last offering had been 29p worth of Value Brand chocolate digestives.

It was easy to fall in love with Freecycle. It was only started in 2003, by Deron Beal, an environmentalist, in Tucson, Arizona. Today, it's huge, with sites in 75 countries. Everything was grist to the mill: I advertised my old books and videos. I got rid of an ancient computer and a set of CDs for learning French. In each case, a flurry of replies was waiting in my inbox as soon as I had offered something. Undoubtedly, living in a big city helped. It was easy to link up with people and pick up or drop things off without adding petrol to the environmental equation.

I was never once let down. Often, things were left outside in a plastic bag for me. I took to hiding wrapped-up items for collectors under our recycling bin in the porch; no need to wait in for them to arrive then. The same names tended to crop up on the postings again and again. I started to meet ardent Freecyclers who were into saving money as well as the planet, just like myself. One or two, when we made a rendezvous to exchange our second-hand treasures, I told about my pound-a-day project. They were the kind of people who were sure to be intrigued; I started getting hints and tips in messages from them. I heard how to use old wellies to make hinges, or repair roof flashing with car inner tubes. Might come in handy one day… They let me know about upcoming free events, offers, newspapers with coupons to collect inside. Furthermore, they bore me in mind if they came across anything they thought would be useful to a pound-a-day survivor. I ate up food for them that was contra-indicated on a post-Christmas diet, or that was just too tempting to have in the house if you wanted to watch your weight!

They didn't just offer comestibles: having heard of my hitching, these thoughtful souls kept an ear to the ground in case anyone was taking a trip with a spare seat in their car. Twice, I was put in the way of train tickets they found they couldn't use by the expiry date. I had a nice day out in Bath without having to cycle there in the cold and the dark. Another time, someone passed on a Day Rider ticket for the bus, early enough for me to take a trip out to Weston-super-Mare and have a bracing walk along the seafront.

My toaster had long ago broken. No problem! I asked if any Freecycler had an old one; the next day I popped into someone's office in town to pick up a model far superior to mine. The couple giving it away had just moved in together and thought it silly to keep a spare. Everyone I met was friendly and generous and green. What a great idea, we all agreed, Freecycle was.

'Do you think anyone would want our old telly?'

Daphne and Martin were munching cheese and biscuits with me, hovering near the wine table, while I enthused about my new-found source of secondhand gems. I had entered a haiku competition, simply because all entrants got to go to a prize-giving ceremony in a local bookshop. To my astonishment, my cynical little verse about sleeping alone had won a prize: a bottle of wine! I was glad I hadn't come first or second, since those entrants were awarded book tokens. I didn't feel I'd be able to justify using them. Drinks, though... It was worth the effort of reading it out for my sixteen seconds of glory.

'I'm sure someone would want it. Does it work?' I asked.

'Nothing wrong with it!' said Martin. 'We've just moved over to a flat screen to save space.'

'But now we've got less space than ever,' laughed Daphne, 'because we haven't got round to going to the tip yet!'

'Tell me a bit about it, then,' I said, fishing a pen from my pocket and folding my haiku printout in half. 'I'll put it online for you tomorrow, to collect only, using your phone number. And one of the great things about Freecycle is that you can screen the replies and give it to the person you think most deserves it, with no need to explain yourself.'

It worked like a dream, they told me. The very next day they answered the phone to a couple who came round and manhandled it into their car, within an hour of the posting. Then they disappointed a dozen more callers. Then they took the phone off the hook. Two more Freecycle converts were now evangelising for the green cause.

129

I had been worried about what would happen if any of my more expensive and important items gave up the ghost. My mobile phone was needing to be charged ever more frequently, and the very cheapest model was considerably more than a quid. And my bike, though running well after its last service, had quite worn brake blocks and tyres. But now, with my new-found community of helpful Freecyclers, I had nothing to worry about. Someone, somewhere out there, would be able to lay their hand on a replacement. Losing things or having them stolen was no longer such a nightmare to contemplate. And I wasn't the only one with limited spending power who was helped out by the site. Ex-homeless people, single parents, refugees, youngsters moving on from living in care, and those who were simply skint, they were all better off from Freecycle. It wasn't just for a bunch of raving greenies. It brought home the fact that everyone benefits from recycling.

A woman joined the office staff at work. She moved, after a month, from a friend's place into her own unfurnished flat. But thanks to Freecycle, it wasn't empty for long: every single thing she filled it with was from a 'wanted' or an 'offered' posting. By choosing the area to collect from carefully, and timing things in blocks, she spent a couple of evenings out in her friend's Volvo and created a very comfortable home. The sense of community the site created got her off to a great start in Bristol: suddenly she had met a whole lot of like-minded people who welcomed her into the fold. As the Americans would say, what's not to like?

April

The most testing time of all: meeting the man of my dreams and agonising over whether to give up the whole, wonderful pound-a-day thing for him...

At last spring was in the air. I had put my watch and alarm clock an hour forward and watched the mornings lightening each day when I opened the curtains. Amazingly, the batteries hadn't run out on my gadgets yet, although I had the option of cannibalising other things if necessary: the TV remote, for instance, had rarely been touched this year. In the evenings, I continued to entertain myself with free events: by dint of volunteering as an usher, I didn't miss the local panto, highlight of the community centre calendar. After leafleting door-to-door in my neighbourhood and putting up advertising material in public buildings, I was rewarded with tickets for the two theatre productions I'd been promoting. And on the streets, day after day, I spotted money, picked it up, and didn't spend it.

I'd at last decided what to do with all that roadkill money. Suggestions from friends had included having a party to mark the end of my pound-a-day year or going on a day-long shopping spree, but that went against the grain of the philosophy I'd been developing. It wasn't just about getting by on a fixed amount of money any more. My outlook was changing. Nowadays, spending money just because it was there seemed pointless and shallow. The marketing people no longer had an influence on my life. I was free! By seeking out the very cheapest of the necessities I bought, I'd learned a lot about the lure of a brand name. Before, I had felt quite snobbish about 'my' brand of shampoo, coffee or margarine. Perhaps it had promised good health, attractiveness or the downright smugness of giving aid to someone in the Third World. Well, I could do my bit for charity without sitting in Starbucks all afternoon. And actually, I felt and looked very well, as my friends noted. Once I discovered how to eat non-fattening cheap meals, I'd ended up in better shape than ever before, without falling for the claims of cosmetics and food marketers who wanted to sell me 'brand ownership'.

Generic products were a revelation: having previously scorned them as inferior rubbish, I was astonished to find that a monochrome label doesn't necessarily mean that you're going to hate the contents of the bottle or can. In Boots, a huge bottle of own-brand deodorant or body lotion cost pennies and did the job. A litre of shampoo, 27p in Asda, kept me going through most of the year. Tesco razors, 16p, are as sharp as anybody's. And tinned and dried staples like sweetcorn, kidney beans, pasta and tomatoes feed you just as well as the big names do. Those TV ads I used to sing along to, I was paying for them! Those colourful layers of packaging that went straight in the bin, my money went with them!

OK, cheap brands do sometimes cut corners. The toilet paper that costs a quarter as much as the posh brands has smaller sheets on a smaller roll. But nowhere near four times smaller! I found myself adopting a shrink-to-fit policy as I downsized on shopping: if I had less of something, I valued it more and used it more sparingly. That's the opposite of what we're supposed to think when promised 3 for 2 or 50% extra free. If something was abundant, I used more of it. Perhaps that's just me, but somehow I doubt it.

So now I was looking at a long-term change in attitude. Going back to my old ways no longer appealed: that coffee-shop habit I used to feed was appalling to contemplate. I couldn't spend my saved-up roadkill money on something frivolous like that.

The only thing to do, then, with all that cash I'd found was to recycle it. I would give it to the most deserving charity I could find at the end of the year. And now I had a goal in mind, I started looking in earnest for the coins and notes which smiled and winked at me from the road day after day.

My bank balance was looking a lot less sorry at last. I was pleased that there was something worthwhile to spend my savings on, and had begun to give some thought to my brother's wedding gift. But what about the things I needed before the big day? I could still only spend a pound every 24 hours until the wedding itself.

To prepare myself for the celebrations to come, I arranged another free relaxation session with soothing Sara. I booked a 'free makeover' at a department store in Cambridge to pamper my skin, and had begged a free cut-and-finish at the hairdresser's where a trainee had cut and coloured my hair earlier in the year.

I'd begun getting emails from Dan and Sarah about their plans. They'd made a hotel reservation for me and my dad, so I'd be able to pay our bill when leaving. I'd go on hitching right up to the day of the ceremony, with my outfit carefully folded away in my backpack. And what about that outfit? Maunagh came to the rescue yet again. She flung open a stack of hat-boxes and shoe-boxes and piled formal wear on her bed until I was quite overwhelmed. I produced the accessories I'd been lent for the big day, and between us we chose the most durable and portable sister-of-the-bride ensemble possible: crushable, crease-proof, rain-resistant and washable. Except for the hat. That was going to be a bit trickier to transport; perhaps I'd have to wear it while hitching! It had to be a dry day in that case...

'You were lucky with the weather, weren't you? Hope it's like that for your brother's wedding!' said Maunagh, holding out a plate of daintily cut pieces of cake. We were at a special book sale day in one of our favourite shops. As yet, we hadn't actually looked at any of the books: the lure of free beverages and nibbles had taken us straight to the comfy chairs of the café area. It was a good chance to catch up after my week away. I had been on my volunteering holiday in Somerset, and returned with plenty to think about.

'It was actually too hot at times. After all that rain we've had, it was lovely being outside in the sunshine!'

'You look like you've been abroad! Come on, tell me what happened. I can see something did!'

I took a sudden interest in stirring my coffee. 'Well, I met a man...'

'I knew it!' Maunagh was on the edge of her seat. 'It's

springtime, you're working on a farm with the lambs lambing and the buds budding and the sap rising – was he another volunteer?'

'No, I was the only one. He was my mentor, showing me what to do,' I grinned. 'But we didn't really get together until the week was over. We got on really well from the start, though.'

'What did you call it? Woofing? What's it about then, and what do you have to do?'

'It's an acronym. It means you're an organic farm volunteer, and you can sign up to do it anywhere in the world where people have joined the scheme through a special website.'

This was the first time the activity centre had tried taking a volunteer. I resolved to be on my best behaviour, since they were just trying out the scheme before committing themselves to joining up. The co-ordinator had welcomed me when I arrived, nicely on time, after hitching from Bristol. After a bit of paperwork, she showed me the little wooden building where I had a room of my own. It was basic, but clean and comfortable, with shared toilets, showers and kitchen. Importantly, there was a washing machine: I expected to be getting pretty dirty, working on the land.

Next she took me on a tour of the site. I was impressed: it was a big place and well-maintained. The kids I saw were having a ball. One group was climbing on a jungle gym, another was harnessed in to a giant game of table football with real live players. If one player wanted to move, his whole line had to go with him.

Smaller kids were sitting in a circle, learning about bugs. And overhead a prolonged whoosh, accompanied by a shriek, announced that somebody was having a go on the zip wire, suspended from a harness and sliding down an overhead cable. Numerous people were working around the grounds; too many names to remember all at once. Then we peeped into the dining room and kitchen, where organic produce from the centre's kitchen garden was being prepared for everybody's lunch. This was where I came in: I would be helping to plant and pick the ingredients for the famously delicious cuisine the centre served.

Outside again, we went across to a circle of wooden benches. The estate staff were having their break in the bright, brittle sun, hot drinks steaming in front of them. A tall man took off his sunglasses and rose to meet us; that was Bruce.

'So you were working with him all week? Or did he just come by now and then to see how you were doing? And what's he like? I'm thinking tanned, broad-shouldered, very green...'

'Yes, he was all that,' I agreed. 'We worked together, six hours a day. That's all I had to do; it wasn't as hard work as I thought.'

'You were lucky then, I mean someone could take advantage if they wanted and work you to death, couldn't they?'

'I suppose so, but this was very laid-back. I didn't really know what to expect. I was kind of thinking I'd be with a lot of other volunteers, maybe locals, or a batch of us all staying at once, like the National Trust do it. But it was nice, being their only Woofer. They were all really pleased to see a new face, and I was a novelty, being the first one they had.'

'But what's this *man* like?' Maunagh was beside herself with impatience. 'He must have been impressive, knowing what you usually think of men!'

She was right. A fair few of our nights out on the town had featured my giving a stinging rebuff to any man who fancied his chances. Maunagh despaired of me: she couldn't understand why I had no time for the dating game.

'He was lovely.' I smiled at the memory. 'I didn't think of him like *that* at all. We just started talking, and never stopped. All the time, we kept finding things we agreed on. And having a laugh together. I don't know where the days went.'

'So he came in under the radar. It's so romantic! There you are, out in the fields together, reaping and sowing side by side…'

'Well, not exactly,' I interrupted. 'But he did teach me a lot, and we did work together. We were picking the salads and things for the kitchen, and planting more seeds, and weeding and digging…'

'But you must have been *filthy* all the time. Was there any chance to get dressed up? Were you wearing makeup?'

'No, I didn't take any. And I could only carry a few clothes.'

Maunagh looked horrified. 'He isn't a crusty sort of a chap, is he? With dreadlocks?'

I laughed. 'Not at all. But all that stuff, dressing up and flirting, it just didn't come into it. We just – we just really *liked* each other.'

A sudden thought struck her. She put down her cake plate with a clatter. 'Did you tell him you were living on a pound a day?'

'Yes, and he was fascinated! That was one of the things that set us off talking, all week.'

'But you can't go out with someone, and only spend a pound a day. Either he'd have to pay for everything, or you'd have to do cheap, boring things, like walks. Or card games…'

'Hang on! You've got us paired off already! I don't even know if I'll ever see him again.'

'You mean you didn't arrange to meet up? Didn't you exchange addresses and things?' Now Maunagh was doubly appalled.

'Well, yes, he's got my number. But I don't know.' I picked at my cake icing miserably. 'He's far away. And like you say, it's not very viable, trying to go on a date when you've only got a pound to spend.'

'But you must! It's *ages* since you took that kind of an interest in a man. And somewhere along the way you must have started to think of him as more than just your mentor.'

'I thought he was gorgeous, as soon as we met. But I was sure he must already be taken. And you remember that one in Englishtown?' We both laughed, thinking back to my frantic emails from a volunteering holiday in Spain. A very tall, very rich, very handsome Spanish man had pursued me ardently all through my week's work there. Luckily, I found out in time that he was also very married.

'Did you ask this guy if he was single?'

'No, but he told me he was divorced while we were working together. We just about knew each other's life stories by last Wednesday.' I sighed and sipped my coffee. It was weird being back in the city again, telling a tale of an adventure that already seemed to be from the distant past.

'So – now what? He's there, you're here. Are you going to make a date and see each other?'

I rubbed my forehead, pushing my sun-bleached fringe out of my face. 'It seems so far away already. And anyway, I don't know if I could face getting into a relationship, even if he lived round the corner. You know my track record with men. It doesn't seem a very tempting prospect, getting into all that all over again.'

'Have you been phoning each other?'

'He's been phoning me. That's another thing. I can only email or do the odd text on a pound a day.'

'Oh, for God's sake!' Maunagh put down her mug impatiently. 'You can't start going out with someone and not spend any money! Come on, it's April already. You're only a few weeks short of a year. Pack it in, get on the train, and get it together with this gorgeous man!'

It was quite a tempting idea. Bruce was calling me every night. We talked like we'd known each other for ages. And we both really, really wanted to meet again. Was I going to pass that up for the sake of a self-imposed challenge? My money was saved, my point was proved. If I was going to meet him again, I didn't want to wait until June. That kind of thing wouldn't wait. But I was stubborn by nature, and reluctant to go back on my pledge to survive a full year through. It might jeopardise a bit of fun with a new romantic interest, but if he was really, genuinely interested, it wasn't going to put him off. Or so I hoped.

'It makes me a bit uncomfortable, Bruce,' I said. 'Like feminism has never existed, and I'm expecting you to take me out and pay for everything. I don't want to do that.'

'OK, well, we don't have to go out for dinner. I'll come over to yours with some food, and we can cook it together.' It was late at night and Bruce and I had been on the phone for an hour. I dreaded to think what all these calls to my mobile were costing him. We were missing each other, though, no doubt about it, and had just about admitted how much we looked forward to our telephone conversations. So now the logical next step was to meet again.

'Look, I'd love to see you,' I said finally. 'Just bring yourself, and I'll get a picnic together. We can go for a walk and catch up. It's so warm, it'll be really nice.'

'Great! Look, I don't want to ruin your challenge. We didn't have to spend anything when we were working together, and look how good that was!'

'Promise me, Bruce, you won't try to take me to the pub, or out for meals or anything. It would be very tempting, but I really want to get through this year and be able to say I've done it without cheating.'

He was laughing now. 'Every man's dream!' he said. 'But maybe you'll let me make up for it, not treating you I mean, later on. It's not that long till June.'

'That's true,' I agreed, feeling a little knot of excitement inside my chest. He wanted to see me in spite my living on a pound a day! And he was hoping we'd still be seeing each other by the end of my year! It would be so easy to get carried away, so easy to cheat and accept his invitations to all the places I admitted I missed: my local pub, nice restaurants, gigs by my favourite bands. I had to keep my head. Suddenly, far from being just around the corner, June was looking very, very distant indeed.

'So what about your picnic? Was it OK? And did you have enough to eat?' asked Maunagh. We were back at the waterfront where we had celebrated in a storm the previous October, after my trip to France. This time it was sunny and still; a beautiful evening to be sitting outside. The yachts moored nearby barely moved in the breeze, and people strolled by in shorts and T-shirts, as if it was June already.

'There was plenty. It took quite a bit of crafty shopping to get everything together though.'

That was an understatement. For the three nights before Bruce came to visit me, I scoured the supermarkets at closing time. Dented tins, dated bread, perishable produce, they all came under my scrutiny. And somehow, from my meagre resources, I produced the makings of a picnic.

'Did he bring anything? I know you told him not to.' She passed the flask over to me, and we poured ourselves mugs of home-made soup. The croutons I sprinkled on the top were little chunks of a stale loaf, toasted in the oven with oil and garlic.

'Yes, he did. He brought wine, and carried everything, and we drank to the success of my challenge. It was a really nice time. He says we have to celebrate properly when my year is over.'

'That sounds keen! He wants to see you again, obviously.'

141

'Yes, it was great. I'm hitching to him next weekend, actually.'

The day of the picnic had mercifully been fine. Under the trees, in a clearing high on the steep sides of the Avon Gorge, Bruce and I laughingly came to a halt, out of breath from the hot climb.

'There aren't many places around here where I don't bump into my students at weekends, but I think we've found one!' I said, surveying the path far below from our eyrie. We sat close together on a log and opened the wine he had brought, a rustic French red.

'It's the same where I live. There's just the main street, so you can't get away from the people you work with, or your neighbours or the local tradesmen. It can take forever to nip out to the shop, because everyone wants to say hello.'

'That's nice though, isn't it? Everybody knows you. But do you find it a bit gossipy there?' I unwrapped a pair of glasses from tea towels, and put the tea towels down as plates on the grass.

'There're one or two terrible gossips around,' he replied, pouring the wine. 'And if I want to have a few drinks, it's better to do it at home. But apart from that, I love it there. It's a good-sized place.'

'I liked it too,' I mused, savouring the robust wine and holding it in the sunlight to enjoy its colour.

'So, come back again,' he said.

I looked up and caught his serious expression. 'You mean, to volunteer? Or to visit you?'

He put down his glass, and took mine from my hand and

put that down too. 'I'd like to see you again. I want to get to know you better.'

It was quite a while before we got around to having something to eat. By the time we did, we were both ravenous, which was just as well, considering the menu on offer.

'Bourbon biscuits and cream cheese. I've never tried this before,' said Bruce, taking an experimental bite of the unusual combination.

The biscuits had been reduced because the pack had split open, and the cream cheese was nearing its sell-by date. There was crusty bread rescued from staleness by garlicky olive oil to dip it in, and a couple of rather elderly iced buns. I had run to a pack of Smart Price tortilla chips and some olives from the deli counter, available in quantities of half a dozen.

I watched a little anxiously as he tucked in to our unorthodox buffet. I was used to this kind of fare, but it was quite another thing to feed it to someone who grew organic food of the highest quality and dined every day in an award-winning works canteen.

'Delicious!' he pronounced. I couldn't help but feel he was being kind, but nevertheless I was relieved. The hospitality had been so wonderful while I was volunteering that I'd returned feeling less like I'd been doing work and more like I'd been entertained in a rural retreat. I wouldn't mind going back to Somerset at all, I decided.

The sun was going down. Reluctantly, we decided to leave. We were a little clumsy as we made our way back down the steep slope. I was tipsy from the wine, and slipped more than once as I followed Bruce back to the path. Losing my footing, I grabbed a tall sapling for balance. There was a sharp crack as it snapped, and he ducked just in time to avoid being hit on the head.

'Oh, no, I've broken it!' I said.

'Good thing it wasn't your leg you broke,' he laughed. 'It's a long way to carry you back home!'

He took my hand and led me through the trees, and before my house was in sight we'd agreed to meet again.

May

Worries about dieting, my changed attitude to shopping, and tips for a money-free life-style.

'It's terrible!' said Bev. 'I need to lose nine or ten pounds, just to get into those jeans I wore at your birthday last year!'

'No problem,' I said, looking up from the chopping board where I was preparing a giant coleslaw. 'Go down to Boots, get out your credit card, and buy a load of their slimming products. They've got loads at the moment, ready for the swimsuit season, as they call it. You could easily lose twenty or thirty pounds just on meal replacement shakes and energy bars.'

'Oh, you're joking,' said Bev after looking puzzled for a moment. 'I meant pounds in *weight*, of course, not in money. But you're right, it's a big industry, relying on people like us who put it on and take it off every year.'

'You've lost weight though, haven't you?' said Maunagh to me, bringing over a red cabbage she had been rinsing at the sink. 'And it can't have cost you much.'

'It was touch and go at the beginning of my year,' I admitted. 'I was eating just in case I couldn't later, and filling up on too many bakery products, because they're so often reduced to 10p or something. But once I got over my fear of being hungry, and recognised how I tend to be greedy when there's a lot of something around, I was okay.'

145

'Well, I wish I could sort my head out,' sighed Bev. 'It's just an endless struggle. And I have spent a fortune on gyms and slimming stuff over the years.'

We were preparing for my birthday party, to be held at Maunagh's with forty or so lucky invitees. We were trying to do some healthy food for the buffet, because so many of our friends were on diets, ready for the summer. The idea of showing off all that flabby winter-white flesh on the beach, in front of hundreds of total strangers, was enough to send the most brazen into a cold sweat. But throwing money at the problem clearly didn't work. How could we avoid getting sucked into the claims of the diet industry?

Virgin Money carried out a survey of dieters which revealed that on average it costs £148 to lose just one pound of fat! Beverley, then, was looking at a potential bill of £1, 480. Predictably, she was less than delighted to hear it.

'Is that true? I won't do it!' she gasped. 'I'll just drink iced water and live on fruit and steamed vegetables. There's still time before we go to Portugal.'

'How about Tae Kwando?' I suggested. 'They offer free trials in Bristol. I've got the freephone number if you want!'

'Or you could get pregnant and then swim for free at all the Council-run swimming pools,' added Maunagh helpfully.

'I think I'll just buy a super-control girdle instead,' sighed Bev.

In the UK, it is estimated, the diet industry is worth a billion pounds a year. Apart from gyms and diet foods, there's also a plethora of slimming clubs to choose from. All of them are out there to cash in on your fears. Then there are hundreds of books detailing plans for a new lifestyle: cabbage soup or no carbohydrate or only carbohydrate or almost no fat… Each of these comes with a hefty section of recipes to send you back to the supermarket and into temptation's way again. You can chart your success – or failure – with numerous gadgets and tools, and hold up the example of your favourite celebrity (who has probably written a diet and exercise plan just for you) to keep you motivated.

At the peak of the Atkins boom, approximately three million people were following this low-carb diet endorsed by a trusted physician. And the low-carb industry is still worth £280 million!

'Dropping' a dress size has become an obsession. If you can't wait, you could pour yourself into a pair of magic knickers for twenty quid or so, or get wrapped from head to foot in some kind of gunk at a health spa. It's supposed to remove inches. It certainly lightens the wallet.

If you can't be arsed to get off the sofa at all, you could spend £40 for the first month's membership of Weightwatchers online. Or you could go to their classes: 6,000 meetings a week raking in revenue of over a million pounds weekly. And their attendance has been growing at 13% a year since 2004!

'What a money-spinner,' mused Maunagh, as she grated up carrots. 'They meet in a church hall, everyone pays a fiver a go, and they just have a couple of part-timers running it, working on commission.'

'And it obviously doesn't work,' added Bev, 'because they all keep coming back!'

'Don't forget all the merchandise,' I put in. 'There's their foods, their magazine, their wine, their scales and stuff for the kitchen…'

'It may seem cynical,' said Maunagh, 'but it seems to me that the whole industry relies on our lack of willpower. If we were all a perfect size ten in our jeans, they'd all be out of a job!'

We were planning to have a vegetarian buffet at my party: it was easier to prepare in advance and to do as a low-calorie feast for the many guests who were on diets. Bruce was coming, too, and he was vegetarian. I wanted him to have something nice to eat after dashing into Bristol after work. Together, our little prep. team made spicy tomato salsa, crudités, fruit salad, guacamole and of course the giant bowl of coleslaw. We had crisps and breadsticks for dipping, and two huge trays of vegetables prepared for roasting. Also, salad stuff sat in the fridge keeping crisp for the last moment. This panoply of fresh stuff was a present from Joy, one of Maunagh's neighbours. She worked in a greengrocer's and got to take her pick of the unsaleable stuff at the end of the night. She didn't often take much, as it was heavy and cumbersome to lug home, but had made an exception for our sakes.

On the day, our party outfits were 'new': the spoils of the naked lady party, teamed with stuff borrowed from one another. I had gone to one of the department stores in town and told them honestly what I was after: full make-up for a special occasion, though I wasn't looking to spend any money that day. I just wanted to see what their products and expertise could do for me. I didn't feel anxious, therefore, that I was going to disappoint the two very nice assistants at the end, and they did an excellent job. We all felt happy at the end of it; I praised their work extravagantly and they beamed with pride.

We had created a warm, understated party venue in the kitchen and lounge. There were tea-lights in jam jars and a scruffy rabble of reduced-price drinks to get people started. I just hoped a few would bring a bottle, as requested on my hand-made invitations.

We needn't have worried. As guests started to arrive, the kitchen surfaces grew crowded with bottles. The noise of talking increased, and I turned up the volume of the music. Luckily, the neighbours were all invited.

Bruce arrived, camouflaged behind a gigantic bouquet of flowers. Everybody said I looked well; what was my secret? He and I shared a smile. Now that the end of my year's challenge was in sight, congratulations were coming in prematurely from all sides. My health and happiness were marvelled upon, my slimness and the smartness of my outfit noted. I was sure that the likes of Bern had expected me to decline into street-person chic by this end of the project. He, to his credit, was happy to eat his words (along with a great deal of free food and wine).

The story of my adventure had got around: my friend who worked for Channel Four wanted to suggest my story to The West Tonight's newsdesk, and a local radio station presenter had also threatened to call early one morning for a live interview. I didn't encourage this kind of publicity:

for one thing, I hadn't finished my year yet, and for another, it was supposed to be a secret way of raising funds for my brother's and his fiancée's present. More than that, it had been a pretty personal journey, in spite of all the help I'd received from generous strangers and friends. I had changed over the course of the challenge: I saw shopping, spending, advertising and acquiring stuff in a totally different light now. It would be difficult to convey how passionately I felt about my new ideas to some stranger eating a ready meal in front of the telly. Even now, I was reluctant to tell my story: the reaction was always extreme and questions were fired endlessly until I called a halt. Although I felt I'd come a long way, it was as much about understanding myself as about recognizing how manipulative marketing strategies can be. Maybe I'd share all this with people one day. But it would be after I'd completed my year and proved my point.

Over by the buffet, Lilli was talking to Janet about her childhood in Slovakia. 'There was no spare money. We just got by with daily needs, and there was nothing left at the end of the week.'

'Discretionary spending just wasn't in my parents' vocabulary,' Janet agreed.

'Even today, when my parents visit and we go to a hotel, they'll pocket the packs of jam, butter and sugar at breakfast as well as all the toiletries from the room!' Lilli laughed.

'And eating out was just an outrageous extravagance, wasn't it? When we went out, we took food with us.'

'My dad wouldn't waste a thing. He recycled everything before there was such a word,' Lilli went on, jingling the ice in her glass. 'He had a boxful of the leather tongues from old shoes, to make patches or hinges with!'

'Well, I vividly remember my mum making new covers for shirt collars from the shirt-tail, and cutting sheets in half to re-sew them with the edges at the centre. Then you could tuck the worn bits in at the sides of the mattress,' said Janet.

'Mine did that too! And then they would be pillowcases, then dusters, then floor-cloths!' said Lilli.

'If I dared leave any food on my plate, my father would tell me that during the war sailors risked their lives to bring us enough to eat. Never mind that that was years before. It was our duty to eat up.'

'It was exactly the same in Slovakia. If someone had dug the land and grown food, and someone else picked it and brought it to market, and my mother carried it home and cooked it, there was absolutely no way we were allowed not to eat it!' said Lilli.

'Therein lies my weight problem,' sighed Janet, reaching for another breadstick.

Bev caught me eavesdropping as I added more salad to the bowl and mixed it in with wooden tongs.

'Have you tried any really blatant blagging this year? Like pretending to be a journalist or something to get into an event?' she asked me.

'I'm ashamed to say I didn't have the guts,' I said ruefully. 'And if I pretended to be a theatre or art critic, I'd be found out in two minutes.'

'I'd be the same – without a glass of wine or two. Then I'd bluff the hind leg off a donkey!' she said.

'I read in the *Guardian Monthly* about someone who pretended to be a freelance magazine writer. She got a Ford Galaxy for the weekend, and loads of Topshop jewellery, just by phoning up the PR companies.'

'Wow! But what if they found out? Would they charge her?'

'I don't know, but I'd be mortified. But being a mystery shopper or diner isn't really that different, is it?' I mused, retrieving my glass of cider from behind a jam jar full of celery sticks. 'You mustn't let on that you work for the company.'

'Did you ever try that? It sounds great!'

'I would've loved to. I checked out the websites, but it's not a part-time thing. It's a proper job. So I couldn't give it a go.'

'Shame. You could really throw your weight around doing that, then rip them to pieces in your report!'

'I did sign up for a few open-forum discussion groups. They wanted the public to put in ideas about the museum, the changes to the NHS, and the waste disposal policy. Oh, and I tested the council's website,' I added. 'All those meetings had buffets and stuff. And it was quite interesting too.'

'How do you get onto things like that?' Bev was intrigued.

'The library's posters and leaflets are a goldmine! If you've got the time to go in, read it all, take notes and follow them up, you can get invited to all sorts!' I said.

'I've heard of people volunteering to test cosmetics at home. You keep all the leftovers,' said Bev.

152

'Yes, I've seen that somewhere. You do a questionnaire online. They haven't got back to me yet,' I said.

'Lots of opportunities online if you know where to look, I suppose.'

'There's so many sites dedicated to freebies! I got nearly all my Christmas presents that way!' I agreed.

'Now you tell me!' said Maunagh, coming over to refill our glasses. 'I thought you'd shoplifted that bag of toiletries you gave me!'

'Did you enter competitions as well?' asked Bev.

'I did, but only the free ones you could enter on the Net.'

'And we scored a couple of nights out from that, didn't we?' said Maunagh.

'A night at the comedy club, that was a good prize. And the tickets to that concert at Colston Hall,' I agreed. 'You've got to watch it on the internet though. I found this amazing site that offered free sweets just for clicking your way through adverts. But as soon as I'd registered my details, I was swamped with junk mail. Serves me right for giving out my address!' I said.

'Those poetry readings were fun, though, in the library and the pub basement,' Maunagh reminisced.

'Did you two ever take part?' asked Bev.

'We did, and we weren't the worst by a long way!' I said, with Maunagh nodding in agreement. 'But I was never brave enough to perform at open mic events, singing or telling jokes in the pubs. Except for karaoke, of course,' I added.

The other two laughed. They knew just how terrible my singing voice was.

'Did you know you can get free tickets for gigs at the Fleece, just by giving out flyers? I only found that one out the other day,' I said.

'It's no good,' said Maunagh, emptying the bottle into our glasses. 'You'll have to do this for the rest of your life now!'

She had hit the nail on the head. I was still learning, even though I was nearing the end of my adventure. There was such a world of opportunity out there for someone with the time, cheek and energy to seek out a money-free lifestyle. How was I ever going to go back to my old, bad ways?'

Bruce came over and we exchanged a special smile. 'Hey, Bruce,' I said. 'How d'you fancy going couch surfing next weekend?'

Hitching in my youth, I'd done my own private version of couch surfing: people had taken me home and put me up as night fell, and I in turn had offered drivers who still had a long way to go the chance to eat, shower or sleep at my shared house near the M1. But that was then, before the World Wide Web. Now, couch surfing had gone global.

I had kept an eye on the Gumtree website for years: it had loads of accommodation ads, ranging from houses to buy to short-term sublets of rented rooms. And yes, ads for couch-surfers. People offered their floor or lounge furniture to others passing through, for the most nominal of fees. Great idea, even though it was all a bit more expensive than a pound. But when I Googled couch surfing, a whole new gamut of opportunity opened up.

A tourist called Casey Fenton had come up with the idea of a community offering free overnight stays after he spammed 1500 Icelandic students to blag a free bed on a trip to Reykjavik. Needless to say, he got one, and a lot more than he bargained for as well. So he started a non-profit company which now has 150,000 members on the books. It was yet another idea I was dying to try out, but now the end of the challenge was in sight. My brother's wedding was around the corner. If I was going to stay true to my word, I'd just have to go on living on next to nothing for a few more weeks, and wait and see what the future would bring after that.

June

Success! I've lived on a pound a day for a whole year, feel better for it, am free of consumer pressures – and in my tiny way have helped save the planet.

Bruce and I were seeing each other every weekend now. What was more, we even found free things to do out in Somerset: I dragged him along to a nearby book launch and to the gala opening of the town's new website. We went to a nearby stately home in the warmth of one evening. It had an admission charge of £6.50 per person, but after six it was closed. And there was a footpath going into the beautiful grounds. All by ourselves, without being bothered by the crowds or indeed by the ticket prices, we enjoyed a couple of hours walking there. Bruce took his binoculars and showed me all the birds on the ornamental lake. We had a great time again, and all for free.

In Bristol, I took him to a performance poetry evening, a free open-air film screening and live street music in the city centre. When we'd have time to go away couch-surfing, I had no idea. But I was determined that going out with someone who lived on a pound a day wasn't going to cost him a fortune.

It was hard sometimes, when he wanted to go to a pub or have a coffee. He, of course, was happy to pick up the tab, but I felt uncomfortable about that. I was more satisfied with a bottle of wine up on a hill in the evening sun or an evening helping to make supper at his house.

In the past, when I'd met someone new, I'd gone on a shopping spree: new underwear, a couple of special outfits to surprise him, a collection of nice fresh makeup. And of course luxurious toiletries and perfumes. But partly because he worked on the land and didn't have much time for that kind of fussy stuff, and partly because he knew about my challenge, it was okay not to covet anything like that this time. He didn't try to buy me presents either, once I'd made it clear that I didn't miss any of those fripperies. In fact, even at this late stage of the year, I still had lots of unused cosmetics and samples from shops and the Internet. And as for sexy undies, they don't get worn a great deal, after all. They're too uncomfortable to go around in every day!

So I rooted through the depths of my clothes collection and found enough variety that I didn't feel bored with the same few outfits all the time. And the best things in life are free, after all: we went for walks, shared our favourite music with each other, showed our photograph collections and treasures, and talked. And talked. Long into the night. I could hardly believe it was going so well: in the past I'd spent money to impress, getting my hair done every Saturday ready for a night out, buying new things to wear just the once, paying for treats and surprises to try and keep things fresh. But this was better. And fresher. We were both having a wonderful time, getting to know each other.

Dan and Sarah extended their invitation to include him, once they heard about Bruce, but we agreed we'd rather meet another time, when we could talk and they wouldn't be so preoccupied. Besides, all the accommodation within miles of the village where they lived had been booked out for months for the wedding, and I was sharing a kind of family suite with my dad, with my bed behind a curtain. Altogether not the ideal way to introduce my new man to the family!

I'd been back up to see my dad, to have him measured up for his suit hire. I was paying for that as well as the hotel, as part of my contribution to the proceedings. Expensive things, weddings.

As for their present, I'd chosen something both easy to carry and unnecessary to pay for in advance. I had a card to give them, with maps and leaflets in a folder, which explained that they were now members of the National Trust for life. I wanted something connected with the environment, and not a possession to try to find room for in their little house. I was pleased the NT was a charity, too. It seemed appropriate to spend my long-saved money in that way.

'But when are you going to tell them?' asked Linda. We had been walking with her new and very energetic springer spaniel puppy, which continued to bounce around us as we sank down exhausted to talk about my trip to the happy event the following week.

'At the beginning, I imagined myself announcing it at the wedding. Or writing it discreetly on their handmade wedding card. Then again, I had an idea I'd say nothing, then drop it casually into the conversation the next time we were reminiscing about that holiday we had in France. But you know what? I'm not going to.'

'You're not going to tell them? Ever?'

'No, it started as a mission to save up for their sakes, but it's turned into something a lot more important than that. I've learned such a lot about myself and my friends, and about human nature in general. I've found out so much about how greediness and waste is messing up people's lives. And messing up the planet as well. I don't want to lay a guilt trip on them anyway, so I'm just going to let them think I'm stingy by nature, and made an exception just this once!'

'I can't believe that,' said Linda. 'You made such huge sacrifices for their sake...'

'But it wasn't really for their sakes after all, you see, it's been so good for me!'

'You do seem happier. Healthier too, I think, and that's without a lot of fancy lotions and potions. Just shows you, doesn't it?'

'I got a lot of exercise, not using public transport. Talking of exercise, how are you getting on, collecting the sponsorship for the marathon you did?'

'Oh, don't talk to me about that!' said Linda, rolling her eyes. 'I feel terrible. I promised the hospice this big amount, and I was so sure I'd be able to raise it from my workmates and the running club and all, but I'm still short. And now it's due in.'

I was rustling around in the pockets of my backpack. At last, I produced a slip of paper. It was a cheque, made out to the total amount of all the money I'd found on the streets over the year: £117.48.

'How do you spell your last name again?' I asked her.

It was drizzling off and on, all the way from Bristol to Cambridge. This was a bit of a disaster for my borrowed wedding hat, since it turned out not to be colour-fast. But it survived without being crushed, tied on to the outside of my backpack, and I survived too. It took a few hours to get down the M4, around the M25, up the M11, and out to the hotel to drop off my things before setting straight off again to my free hair and makeover session in town. Mercifully, by then the rain had stopped, and I decided that if I slept very carefully, and didn't rub my eyes too much, I'd be able to preserve most of the effect for the morning. I had my own make-up to touch things up with, but felt a bit strange hitching in a full coat of slap out to a rather nice hotel!

My dad and a few other relations had turned up. Luckily, they were all tired from travelling, so there were no plans for a big night out. Although I could have paid for things on the hotel tab, it didn't seem right somehow to be going into debt on the very last day of my year's challenge.

It was harder still not to tell anyone. I felt euphoric: so excited to have made it without cheating, to have saved up and reached my goal, and to have kept it secret all this time from the entire family. It was highly tempting to raid the minibar or spill the beans, or both. Well, I thought, if I did one I'd probably end up doing the other, so instead I invited my cousin out for a walk. A red sunset heralded fine weather for the morning, and after a chat in our little suite with a few of the other relations I hadn't seen for years, I pulled the curtain to divide off my little room and went to bed.

I haven't been to a lot of weddings, but from my limited experience, it seemed like a very nice one. A group of us took a minicab – what luxury! – to the dear little chapel where Dan and Sarah were to be married. I smiled to myself and wondered whether I'd ever hitch again. For sure, I decided: it was such a nice way to travel. Private hire vehicles are so impersonal by comparison.

I was wearing my special outfit, the fruit of my friends' collaborative labours. I remembered how much fun we'd had sorting it out before I set off: Maunagh's clothes, Penny's shoes, Janet's bag and jewellery. Would it have been the same, going to a personal shopper in Debenham's or somewhere? I doubted it.

A cluster of guests were chatting on the lawn when we arrived at the chapel. It must be earlier than I thought: nobody had gone in to sit down yet. Then I heard, to my alarm, that thanks to the wonders of mobile phone technology, it had been discovered that Dan hadn't arrived yet. His bride-to-be was driving round and round until he did.

This was slightly disturbing. Surely he hadn't got last-minute cold feet? Not his style at all. His best man, I remembered, was a bit of a scatterbrain: had he forgotten the ring or something? Or overslept and forgotten to wake Dan up? I tried their mobile numbers, and found they were switched off. Sensible really. A ringtone going off in the middle of the solemnities would really put them off. But what on earth had happened? People were looking slightly anxiously at their watches. Luckily, my dad hadn't yet realised anything was amiss; my aunty was keeping him fully occupied with small talk.

A ripple went through the crowd. Was this them? But it couldn't be. They had borrowed a lovely old Bentley for the

161

day, and this was just a people-mover pulling into the driveway. Then my brother waved from the passenger seat, and a frisson of relief ran through the guests. My brother and his best man jumped out and straightened their tailcoats, and Dan grinned at me.

'The wedding car broke down!' he said. 'We've just had to hitch-hike!'

This is the point at which all the Happily Ever Afters started. The bride arrived, traditionally well after the groom, and Dan and Sarah had a beautiful wedding. So far, they've also had a beautiful life together. They've been visiting National Trust properties and having fun with their present, and they've never discovered how I paid for it.

Bruce invited me to live with him, not very long after all of that. So I became an English teacher who lives in the country and bakes her own bread. I decided to write the story of my year, in the hope that people might find a bit of inspiration when they've got something expensive to save for, or debts to get rid of, or if they just feel like they're getting too tangled up in the culture of shopping. It feels good, being free of all that consumer pressure. It helps to save the planet too, and maybe you might want to give it a try just for that.

My life changed pretty drastically once I moved to a small Somerset village, but I'm still in touch with all those wonderful friends who stood by me through thick and thin. People are what it's all about, really. You're nothing without them.

And yes, I still find it very hard to spend more than a pound a day.

The following pages give website addresses and advice to help you to live on a pound a day – at least now and then!

Holidays and Trips

www.wwoof.org
This is the website for organic farm volunteers in places worldwide, such as the farm below:

www.sussexcountryretreat.co.uk

www2.btcv.org.uk/display/btcv_home
The BTCV organises volunteering days out in the country.

www.vaughanvillage.com
Free holidays in Spain and Italy, staying in high standard hotel resorts, just speaking English to people who want to learn! I've done this in several locations and had a wonderful time. It really is free – you just get yourself to the meeting point (airport or city centre nearest to the resort) then everything else is paid for.

House sitting
Advertise, ask around, look on the web: companies who do this may either ask a small fee of the house-sitter or pay them to do it! It's a great way to get free accommodation and have fun in a new area.

www.gti-home-exchange.com
If you've got your own place, Green Theme International will help you to swap it for someone else's (for £25 a year membership) almost anywhere in the world, for short or long periods. I've never owned a house so haven't tried it out but friends who have say it's a great idea. There are lots of similar sites out there.

Camping 'wild'
That's what they call it in Germany. It means camping for free in a remote place where you won't bother anyone. Ideally nobody should even know you're there. I've done this in a few secret locations. The vital thing is to leave no trace of your presence behind.

www.couchsurfing.com is the gateway to free accommodation and an entertaining experience with your hosts besides!

Entertainment

Many of these 'leads' are Bristol-based but there are similar opportunities in every town and city in the country.

www.bathfringe.co.uk
Street entertainers, parades and much more.

www.bristol.ac.uk
The University of Bristol, along with UWE and most other UK universities, has a programme of events open to the public. Just have a look on their websites: lectures, tours, open days and arts and music events happen throughout the year.

Open studios and art trails offer many pleasurable hours. You get to nosy in other people's houses along the way, and see streets you'd never otherwise bother walking down.

Tourist information in your own city, from a tourist office or online, gives valuable hints on things to do. Don't take your home town for granted. It's right there to enjoy without incurring any travel costs or overnight stays.

Themed city walks are a good way to learn more about your own patch. Get fit and meet people at the same time: they're usually run by local enthusiasts with an impressive knowledge of their subject. I've learned lots about architecture, slavery and the Bristol riots on walks like these.

Dog walking for the RSPCA or other charities is always needed. What better way to take some exercise than with a grateful furry friend?

Events

www.fleecegigs.co.uk
Go to 'Street team' link for free tickets in return for distributing flyers. An even better scheme runs at:
www.tobaccofactory.com/html/theatre_supporting_us.htm

www.bristolfiesta.co.uk This is the site for the free annual Bristol balloon fiesta at Ashton Court.

www.kite-festival.org.uk/visitor-info At Bristol's Ashton Court, like the balloon fiesta, well worth a visit.

www.visiteastside.co.uk/events_calendar St. Marks Road, Bristol street party, art trails and more!

www.poetrycan.co.uk Free poetry events all over the place.

www.poetryarchive.org/poetryarchive/home.do This site helps you if you want to organise a poetry event of your own, wherever you live. It also offers lots of downloadable material to write in home-made greetings cards or just pass on to friends.

'Almost-free' theatre tickets are available in London. Look on: www.royalcourttheatre.com/bookingdetail.asp?ArticleID=3

'Standing' seats are available at 10p! They are restricted view, but still a cracking deal. They are available if you go in person, one hour before performance, to the Jerwood Theatre Downstairs at the Royal Court Theatre.

www.londonforfree.net A list of free stuff and links to lots more in the capital and beyond.

www.flashmob.co.uk If you want to see a really hilarious free spectacle, and perhaps take part in it yourself, have a look at this: flash-mobbing goes on everywhere!

www.bookcrossing.com To pass on books and track their progress around the world, this is a fun, free way to amuse yourself. And if you don't find any books lying around from them, don't forget the wealth of resources at your library.

Libraries

Not just books but new magazines and papers, maps, internet, events, noticeboards of hundreds of more things to do and see, and cheap music and film rentals. Probably lots more too that I haven't mentioned: my local library does a book club, poetry readings, kids' and babies' clubs and exhibitions with talks and tours. Via the library I've discovered shop opening events, gala days, jumble sales, memorial lectures, free concerts, book launches and study and discussion groups.

On the street

Read every notice, be it in a shop window or tied onto a lamp-post. There could be something there for you! Take every leaflet you're handed and stop to talk to everyone with a clipboard. In this way I recently got invited to a discussion on supermarkets with a reward of £30 in vouchers, and I've always found free hairdressing through the ads in salons, wanting people to volunteer to help their trainees. Oh, and look out for coins and even notes dropped from careless fingers...

Museums and galleries

Free admission, entertainment, special events. Great! Get on their mailing lists if possible: ask at their reception desk. Private galleries and art schools also have openings with nibbles and a glass or two of wine: check noticeboards or 'what's on' guides in the larger ones, and ask the staff in smaller ones. It's worth reading the noticeboards in public or semi-public buildings wherever you go: opportunities are all over the place.

Trawling the internet
Try Googling your town or city and adding 'free event' or a date and 'free'. The tourist information websites for a city have useful links too.

Newspapers still have stuff worth reading long after the day they are published. Look in recycling bins or ask people to save you theirs. Free papers like the *Metro* have pointed me in the direction of all kinds of entertainment and events. Supermarket magazines are often free as well, and contain coupons and recipes. My rule is: take anything that's handed to you!

Coupons from newspapers or elsewhere are well worth cutting out. 'Token collect' offers can be amassed without ever buying the product with the tokens on it: I once went to see a Tina Turner concert after collecting chocolate wrappers discarded on the street, and sending off for a ticket.

Tasting sessions at wineries, foodstores etc. are good opportunities to invite your friends to something when you're broke. The same goes for shop openings, book launches, art openings and 'anniversary' promotional events in public buildings.

Children's events are often fun for older people and usually have free or reasonable admission: special museum days, wildlife walks and film shows are just some examples.

'Doors open' days in many towns provide access to sites of interest usually inaccessible to the public. In some areas, there's even a free bus to take you to the more distant sites, which might include a tour of such things as water treatment works, historic houses, architectural landmarks or an archaeological dig.

Car boot sales can provide a lot of fun for the browser or the seller. Choose one without an entry fee.

Local sports events are fun if the weather's OK. You could even join in...

Market research has come a long way since a woman with a clipboard kept you standing in the rain. Nowadays you may well be ushered into a cosy church hall to do your survey seated at a laptop. Incentives are offered too: I've received coffee, chocolate or shopping vouchers for my efforts, as well as making the day of the person trying to get people to take part!

Free-to-enter competitions may provide a nice surprise if you are one of the lucky ones. Plenty of these are online or in magazines and newspapers, and I've been lucky more than once. Just beware of the spam or junk mail that may follow: always tick the 'no' box asking if you will allow further correspondence.

Churches are full of nice things to do, whether you're religious or not. They offer 'all welcome' invitations to concerts, suppers, recitals and talks, and frequently hold them in historic buildings with superb architecture.

Schools of music have free concerts too, and they're often excellent.

Streets have buskers, art shows, window shopping, Christmas lights, parades... It's worth taking a walk downtown. Of course Bristol has Banksy-spotting too. Shopping malls sometimes put on entertainment as well, out of the weather.

In the country (which can be surprisingly close to a city's fringes) there are opportunities to try your hand at wildlife and bird watching. Take a field guide and some binoculars to get more out of it.

Test drive cars just to see what they're like, and you'll often get a free gift for doing so.

Foreign language social groups often advertise for new members or guests: practise your holiday French and meet some interesting people over a buffet of regional snacks.

Firework displays aren't just on November 5th. And you don't have to go in to the venue to enjoy the show! The same goes for many concerts: you can appreciate them nearly as well from outside!

Films Go to seefilmfirst.com/homepage.welcome.action This explains how to register to see free films.

www.showcasecinemas.co.uk Here you can see new films for free or enter competitions to win tickets etc. You have to register though.

www.freecinematicketsuk.co.uk This site promises you 'One free night out a week' which can't be bad. Especially if you have to find seven free nights out every week.

TV show audiences have a lot of fun. There's usually food and drink and sometimes transport provided. Try www.channel4.com or www.endemol.com for current shows. Don't forget radio shows also recruit audiences. And how about being a contestant on a game or quiz show? The websites above tell you how to apply.

Volunteering

www.do-it.org.uk/
UK-wide opportunities for volunteers in all kinds of roles.
The British Trust for Conservation Volunteers has groups going out daily across the UK. Transport and equipment, and a hot drink, are provided.
'Friends of' groups support parks, monuments, churches, public buildings and other places which need a bit of maintenance. There are all kinds of opportunities to help out. Try looking up a site near you online and seeing if there's a volunteering programme for it.

www.naturenet.net/people/volunteers.html

Details of National Trust volunteering are on this website. You do have to pay for the privilege of working for them, though food and accommodation is provided.

Free training

Try putting your city name and 'free training' into Google. This opens up quite a few intriguing avenues in your area.

Ushering at your local arts cinema, concert hall or theatre usually gets you free tickets for other shows, and you may well see most of the one you're working at.

Psychology and other experiments at your local university require volunteers, who are usually paid a token amount for their time (£5-£10 on average). They don't tend to involve much more than doing some matching or speaking exercises on a laptop for an hour or less. Other departments, such as Medicine, also ask for individuals to help out: see university noticeboards for details.

Medical guinea pigs are always in demand: see the www.gpgp.net website or the Common Cold Research Centre for details. They offer money or other incentives for what isn't necessarily an unpleasant experience!

Transport and travel

Hitching is still possible in this day and age. Allow plenty of time, carry a map and a mobile phone for emergencies, and hold up a sign to show where you want to get to. Stand in a sensible place where people can see you and pull over to pick you up. Look respectable and clean, wear light colours, and don't take a lot of luggage.

Walking is very under-rated. What is so terrible about walking home with your shopping? Put it in a backpack and save plastic bags. Get fit and reduce carbon emissions! Walking for pleasure is much enhanced by the many footpaths around Britain. There are excellent books which can be borrowed from the library, guiding walkers around your area to places you never knew existed.

Bicycles will save you a packet and a lot of time too. Look up the 'Bike Doctor' for free bike servicing at community events.

Free buses are sometimes laid on to the supermarket, mall or bingo hall. You don't have to go in there or spend money when you arrive...

Have a look at the following sites too:

www.mylifts.com Attempting to pair up drivers and people seeking lifts.

www.carshare.com A directory of car-sharing sites in the UK.

www.gumtree.com Look under 'travel partners' on the site for your city (via the 'other cities' link). Gumtree has lots of other good stuff too, including couch surfing, jobs, freebies and giveaways of all kinds.

www.freewheelers.com You have to register and spend a fair bit of time trying to match journey, driver and passenger. I haven't had success with this yet, but will keep on trying.

www.megabus.com A quid to London from Bristol can't be bad. There's a 50p booking fee payable once no matter how many tickets you book at a time. There's also www.megatrain.com with services in the UK and elsewhere.

www.234car.com/bikebuddies/bikebuddies.html This is the site for people who want a 'bike buddy' to cycle within Bristol: to work or anywhere else, while www.bikebudi.com does the same thing nationally.

Frugal lifestyle support

The Transition movement aims to improve a community's sustainability and reduce its dependence on fossil fuels. See if your town is involved yet.

www.freegan.info The Freegans are really into frugal living and consider their cause a political statement. Interesting reading.

Local Agenda 21 groups support people who want to get busy with sustainable living. Check the Web for details of meetings in your area.

The Compact in San Francisco will give you inspiration and you can join up wherever you are. Look at: www.groups.yahoo.com/group/thecompact

www.buynothingday.co.uk is a great site with a great idea. In the USA the day not to spend is straight after Thanksgiving. Watch their space for when it is here.

To chat about all things free:
www.freecycle.org/faq/manual/mod_cafe will show you how to set up a Freecycle café forum. There are some good ideas out there!

www.downshiftingweek.com shows you how to downsize and declutter. You don't need all that stuff, and you're just working to keep it all cluttering up your life!

If you've got to buy something new, there are loads of price comparison sites to help you find the cheapest. Go to www.paler.com/price_comparison for a comprehensive list of these UK sites.

Free samples can be tracked down at: www.free-stuff.co.uk and lots of other freebie sites too. Quite good fun waiting for the postman to come slogging up the drive.

Food and drink

Foraging can be fun. In season, look out for hazelnuts – if you can beat the squirrels to them! Best roasted before cracking. Chestnut trees are all over the place and provide pleasing roasted nuts or an ingredient for stuffing. There are lots of apple, pear and plum trees on wastelands or roadsides with fruit going to waste: why not pick it and use it? Same goes for blackberries etc. If you're brave enough, go mushrooming: preferably with an expert, or if not with a good identification guide.

Lots of edible leaves are out there for the picking in different terrains, including watercress, dandelion, nettle and sea spinach.

How about having a go at river or sea fishing? Or hunting for shellfish or crabs?

If you have a garden, consider turning some of it over to vegetables. Swap seeds with friends or get your own from tomatoes etc. Sprouting potatoes, when planted out, produce a decent crop of new spuds without having to buy seed potatoes.

If you haven't got a garden you can still grow herbs or tomatoes on the windowsill. You could offer to do gardening for someone else in return for a share of the produce.

Hens are easy and cheap to keep if you have the space and a secure, foxproof run. You can get free ex-battery hens all over the country by contacting www.bhwt.org.uk (the Battery Hen Welfare Trust) and expect a plentiful supply of eggs to follow.

Tasters in shops are a lovely bonus while you're out and about, and sometimes they give you samples to take home. Health food shops seem to be the best, and may give you tea bags or other tasters to try later. Shop openings are worth looking out for too. Street markets or fairs, especially farmer's markets, are keen on giving out tasters of their wares, and supermarkets or food halls promoting a product will often be handing out nice little snacks to try. Look out for new products advertised on TV, billboards or newspapers. There will often be a website where you can get a sample posted to you, or a coupon for a free pack of the promoted item. Newspapers often have a token-collect offer with a free item for every reader once you've saved up enough coupons, published daily. If it's a local paper, and the newspaper office is near you, the policy is to give out one coupon per day per person if you ask at reception. (These have to be 'no purchase necessary' offers by law.) So you don't even have to buy the paper!

Open days are regularly held by all kinds of public buildings, and snacks and drinks are often provided to tempt people to hang around. There's a phone shop in Bristol, for instance, which has a 'help-yourself' coffee machine to enhance your browsing. And if you enter a bank, salon or department store which is having a marketing event, you may well leave clutching a goody bag. I came out of a local optician's with an umbrella and a travel alarm clock recently, just for looking round the premises.

Bargains in the supermarket tend to be put out an hour before closing time, particularly in the deli and bakery sections. Look out, however, for the grocery 'whoops!' shelf with dented tins and things nearing their sell-by dates, and the section of the fridges which contains reduced-to-clear fruit and veg. and chilled foods. It's worth popping in to check these areas out whenever you're passing and have the time. Stock up the freezer or cupboard whenever you can for leaner times: tinned and frozen goods can spin out a dish of fresh ingredients nicely. Deli counters are good too: you can ask for just a little sliver of cheese, or five or six olives. No waste and much cheaper than buying lots. If you see a 'try me free' offer on a package, read the conditions, buy it, and send in the wrapper with proof of purchase. A cheque will arrive in due course. If you just remember to send the wrapper in, that is… And most supermarkets have a 'love it or return it' policy. If you don't love it, say so and get your money back. Complain if you think it's justified. It's your money. On the other hand, always be polite and understanding with retail staff. It's a horrible job. And they do remember faces.

In the greengrocer's, there is usually a 'reduced' box somewhere near the till. They may be amenable to sweeping the whole of its contents into your shopping bag if you bargain with them.

Old-fashioned butcher's shops have bones and other scraps for free or almost free. And if you happen to know a fishmonger's, they will give you heads and other scraps to make delicious soups and stocks.

Packed lunches save money and time. They also prevent over-indulgence when you're hungry and temptation comes your way! A flask is a good idea, but takeaway cups of cold or hot water are usually given for the asking at fast-food places, motorway rest stops or big, canteen-style restaurants. So you don't need to carry one unless you're out in the wilds or you really want to. And all chain-style pubs, and most privately run ones, offer free glasses of tap or soda water, or a glass of ice.

Mystery shoppers If you're interested in being a 'mystery shopper' in pubs and restaurants, have a look at: cybershop.gfk.com which tells you how to apply. You get paid to shop! And eat and drink for free! Wow.

Discussion groups on a huge range of topics are often advertised locally by market research companies or government bodies, or members of the public are invited to government events to observe or participate. These almost always involve a reward: coupons, a buffet, or a contribution towards your travel and time.

Waste isn't an option for someone living on a pound a day. You can turn excess food into dried, pickled or frozen versions, make breadcrumbs or croutons from stale bread, invite people round to help you eat stuff up, or just give it away. Soup can be made from scratch with stalks and leaves and all manner of leftovers, using stock saved after cooking potatoes or steaming vegetables. Or as a last resort, Freecycle is a good place to give or receive unwanted food as well as almost everything else.

Food For Free by Richard Mabey (Collins, first published 1972 but still in print) gives lots of advice on how to forage for fodder!

Household

Websites of products you'd like such as www.dove.co.uk often yield questionnaires which reward you with samples.

Jumble and garage sales are rich sources of bargains, especially as closing time draws near. Car boot sales are a fun morning out too. www.freecycle.org is great for furniture, clothing, cleaning products, etc.

Small ads in shop windows sometimes offer items cheaply or for free. The small ads in the newspapers have a 'freebies' section too.

Vacuum cleaner bags can be re-used many times. It's not a nice job but just put on the Marigolds and fish out the contents of the bag. Carefully!

Skills exchanges operate in a great number of communities now. People offer to fix stuff, do household chores, baby- or pet-sit etc., in return for other help. If you can't find a local group, start your own among your friends.

Lost property, if handed in to the police, becomes yours after a few weeks if unclaimed.

Plants, branches and leaves picked from the hedgerows make beautiful free decorations for your table or around doorways etc. Conkers are said to keep spiders away, and they look nice in a bowl too. Pine cones, bulrushes, dried wild flowers and grasses all make pretty displays.

178

Old clothes and textiles can be re-used endlessly: old sheets can be 'turned' and re-hemmed to give a new lease of life, then converted into pillowcases. They could be dust sheets while decorating, curtain liners, dusters or floor cleaning cloths. Pretty fabric scraps can be cut with pinking shears to make ribbons for wrapping gifts or flowers, or for your hair. Long-sleeved tops convert easily into funky bags: sew the sleeves together at the cuffs and join them to make the shoulder bag handle, then sew up the hem. You put your shopping in the neck opening! Stuff sleeves or trouser legs with other scraps to make draught excluders, and make your own cushions. Odd socks, slipped over your hand, make dusting tricky places easy.

TV is unnecessary. Make the most of the radio or internet. If you do get to watch telly, it will be a special occasion, like going to the cinema, and you're much more likely to be discerning in what programmes you choose. You'll get a lot more done without it, and although the TV licensing authority will still threaten you forever, you will at last be free of an expensive bill.

Swap clothes, accessories and jewellery, books etc... You could do it among friends or advertise an event at your workplace. See www.swishing.org for ideas.

Envirofone have a website through which you can recycle your old mobile phone for cash. Not to be sneezed at: they even pay the postage.

Firewood doesn't have to be bought: get it from skips, the beach, the woods or from friends. You could have a woodburner, an open fire or a focus for a winter party in the back garden, with candles in jars, fairylights in the window, and hot potatoes to keep everybody warm.

Friends and Family

Don't neglect them: they're the most important support network you'll ever have.

Give away recipes, books, websites, newspaper cuttings etc. If you see something a friend would be interested in on TV, video it for them. You have a great resource which doesn't require spending money: your invaluable time!

Presents are a good idea any day of the week. Home-made ones are much appreciated: how about biscuits or cakes?

Charity shops have bric-a-brac which can make a nice gift when cleaned up and nicely wrapped.

Wrapping paper is of course saved from everything else you've received. Flower wrappers look pretty on presents, and there is often a ribbon to re-use.

Cards can be hand-drawn, printed from a photo or a picture from your PC, or appliquéd from a collection of bits and bobs around the house. The message inside can be poached from an online poem, or write one yourself.

Postage is expensive. Send stuff by email, impersonal as it is, or even better hand-deliver if possible. If not, use second class post: everybody knows it arrives just as slowly as first!

Make wish or gift lists for friends. They don't have to contain material things: what about a babysitting session so you can go out somewhere, or help cleaning or mending something?

Share appliances and tools. Pass things on when no longer useful to you, for example magazines, clothes and toys. Kids tire of stuff fast and I tire of kitchen gadgets fast: how long do I need that yogurt maker or string bean slicer cluttering my cupboard?

Fix things for each other. I'm good at putting filler in holes in walls and repainting them, for example. But since I'm bad at sewing, I can do a spot of DIY in return for getting something altered for me.

Evenings out with friends and relations don't have to put you out of pocket. Offer to arrive with a box of ingredients for dinner, cook them for everyone, and produce a DVD to watch afterwards. Oh, and then wash up...

Safari parties are an extension of the same idea: you all go for one course at one house, dessert at the next, and drinks before and after at other places again. It's better and cheaper than a pub crawl.

Picnics are great in any season. You can turn out to the park for lunch in the depths of winter with hot baked potatoes and soup and a flask of hot chocolate and have an enjoyable time getting some fresh air.

Your own book club (or art group or yoga session) is free in someone's house or garden.

Help each other with the daily boring stuff. What about having a weekly house-cleaning blitz group where 3 or 4 people spend an hour working on the house of one of the group, then all sit down for coffee?

Bookshops often have an area with comfy chairs for browsers. They're a great place to meet and sit for a chat in town. Do buy occasionally (my publisher insists!).

Swap childcare or pet-sitting. Why pay someone else when it works out better in every way to do it yourselves?

Day tickets for the bus and train are officially non-transferable. But they can be used on as many journeys as you like before you get tired and pass them on to a friend to dispose of for you.

Offer lifts or to do errands if you have to go somewhere in private transport. Ask for lifts if you know people of your acquaintance make a journey to somewhere you'd like to go.

Pay-as-you-go mobiles mean you don't have to worry so much about getting a phone stolen. You'll use it less if it's inconvenient to top it up. And it doesn't hurt to ask friends if you can make a call on their mobiles or landlines when they have an offer of 'free minutes' or texts to use up.

Personal care

Trainees often need guinea pigs: dental schools and alternative practitioners advertise in newsagents' and small ads for people to be practised on for free, usually with a qualified person in attendance.

Hairdressers and beauticians post 'models wanted' notices in their windows; be sure to ask if there is a charge though.

Colleges and training academies which do beauty and hairdressing courses have cheap prices for treatments anyway but they too give freebies from time to time.

Open days at gyms, hotel spas and therapy rooms are a good way of spending a luxurious few hours trying out their facilities.

Taster sessions in reflexology or many other techniques are often offered in health food stores or alternative treatment rooms.

Makeovers in department stores or cosmetics shops will give you a lift and make you feel like a million dollars (just make sure they know you're not out to spend anything like that much!).

Generic brands of medicines and toiletries in pharmacies are much cheaper and usually just as good as the brand-name items.

Prescriptions are often handed out willy-nilly. They cost a lot. Ask the pharmacist if something cheaper will do, or decide for yourself if you really need all the items your doctor has written out for you: you don't have to have them all if you don't want.

Mini toiletries are frequently handed out as samples. They're ideal for going away for the weekend; you can ask for samples online by going to the websites of many of the big cosmetics companies. You can always refill the containers to make your own weekend kits.

Shoes last longer if you change them frequently. This also eases fatigue; someone living on a pound a day walks a lot! You could, for example, keep a spare pair or two at work, and wear scruffier ones to and fro, keeping the 'best' ones looking respectable.

Water is free and it's very good for you. Carry a very small bottle (because of the weight and bulk of the things you're carrying) but fill it and drink from it frequently while you're out and about.

Exercise books and videos will keep up your interest in fitness. Share them with friends and get new ones from the library. Do the exercises with other people, in the garden, in the park, or with the kids. Make it fun. You could learn massage from books or videos too and give your friends a treat.

Free samples for presents (or just to treat yourself) can be tracked down at: www.free-stuff.co.uk and lots of other freebie sites too. Quite good fun waiting for the postman.

To help you save up for a treat for yourself or others, http://forums.moneysavingexpert.com give good advice and links to other resources.

Also look at www.greasypalm.co.uk: sign up and you'll be bombarded with offers of freebies.

Books

The following are well worth a look perhaps in the library, buying or just 'browsing' in the bookshop...

Not Buying It: My Year Without Shopping by Judith Levine (Free Press, 2006)
Mr. Thrifty's How to save Money on Absolutely Everything by Jane Furnival (Michael O'Mara, 2003)
Smart Saving Tips by Jane Furnival (Hay House, 2007)
Teach Yourself Thrifty Living by Barty Philips (Hodder Education, 2007)
Food for Free by Richard Mabey (Collins, first published 1972)